ON FIRE WITH THE SPIRIT

On Fire with the Spirit

John Bertolucci

with
Fred Lilly

SERVANT BOOKS
Ann Arbor, Michigan

Published by Servant Books
P.O. Box 8617
Ann Arbor, Michigan 48107

Cover photo by John B. Leidy © 1984 Servant Publications
Cover and book design by John B. Leidy

84 85 86 10 9 8 7 6 5 4 3 2 1

Printed in the United States of America
ISBN 0-89283-193-6

Library of Congress Cataloging in Publication Data

Bertolucci, John.
  On Fire with the Spirit.

  1. Christian life—1960·   2. Holy Spirit.
I. Lilly, Fred.   II. Title.
BV4501.2.B43 1984   248.4   84-5413
ISBN 0-89283-193-6 (pbk.)

This book is dedicated to the bishops and presbyters of the Diocese of Albany, New York, who share with me the greatest fraternity in the world: the priesthood of the Catholic Church. In particular I wish to honor Bishop Edward Maginn, Bishop Edwin Broderick, Bishop Howard Hubbard, Father Walter Czechowicz, Father John Mosconi, Father John Malecki, Father Bertrand Fay, Father Edward English, Father Crispin Fuino, O.F.M. Conv., the late Father Henry Tansey, M.H.M., Father Michael Scanlan, T.O.R., and the many other brothers who were always there when I needed the ministry of the saving and healing Lord.

Contents

Preface / ix
Introduction / 1
1. The Holy Spirit Rushes In / 9
2. Anointed to Preach / 23
3. Living Each Day in the Spirit / 35
4. A Spirit of Power / 45
5. Personal Evangelism / 61
6. Called to Be Saints / 75
7. The Call to Television / 87
8. FIRE / 95
9. Knowing God Loves You / 109

Preface

I REMEMBER VIVIDLY the first time I heard Father John Bertolucci preach. I was attending a large Christian conference; he was one of the main speakers. It had been a long, full day. I was exhausted and my mind had received far more teaching than it could handle. Father John was the last speaker.

Since I was sitting toward the front of that huge arena, I could see Father John plainly, and it was obvious that he was anxious to begin his talk. I, on the other hand, was anxious to go home.

Apparently, I was the only one who felt that way. As Father John was introduced, the people sitting near me began to stir with enthusiasm. They knew something I didn't. They knew that no matter how tired they were, or how full their minds were, the inspired preaching of Father John Bertolucci would set them on fire. They knew he would inspire them to leave the conference filled with zeal to live for God. How right they were!

After the introduction Father John bounded up to the podium and immediately launched into an enthusiastic speech. He didn't even take time to warm up—he just started talking as fast as he could. "Hold your applause," he said, "I only have thirty minutes, and I have a lot to say to you."

In that half hour he said a great deal. My feeling of exhaustion melted away as I became caught up in the vitality of Father John's speaking style and in the solid, practical wisdom he was offering. Here was something I could take home and put into practice.

Hundreds of thousands of people have had similar experiences of the preaching of Father John Bertolucci, either at conferences or on radio and television. But how many know the man himself? How many of us really understand the basic principles that guide his life and ministry?

Father John asked me to help him write this book so that many of these questions could be answered. Our purpose was to present Father John's testimony in a way that would inspire Christian people to seek after Jesus Christ with fervor; to burn with zeal for God. If anyone can inspire Christian fervor and zeal, it is Father John Bertolucci.

I have spent many months following Father John around the country, listening to tapes of his sermons and speeches, and interviewing the people he works with most closely. I have discovered a man of wisdom, a man of compassion, a man of extraordinary personal integrity. Father John Bertolucci is a priest who lives a life of selfless dedication to the great commission, to spread the gospel of Jesus Christ because he knows that "there is no salvation in anyone else; for there is no other name in the whole world given to men by which we are to be saved" (Acts 4:12).

Fred Lilly

Introduction

"How beautiful upon the mountains are the feet of him who brings glad tidings" (Is 52:7).

I CAN CLOSE MY EYES and see them—beautiful deep blue mountains, framed against a sky of bright blue. These are the Catskills, mountains that have loomed large in my life for as long as I have had memory.

I was born beneath their shadow in Catskill, New York. I remember as a child gazing steadily out my bedroom window at those mountains, which seemed to dominate everything I saw. And I remember also many trips through those high and scenic hills with my father. Even to this day, though I have travelled far and wide in the service of Jesus Christ, I am most at home when I'm fortunate enough to be in the Catskills.

As for my feet, which may have been beautiful when I was a child, they are now aging and calloused by long hours of standing, an occupational hazard for one called to the ministries of preaching and teaching.

As I look back over my life, probably more than half over at this writing, I can identify all the events and influences that shaped my destiny. The story of

1

how the Holy Spirit came rushing in—to change forever the plans of a man whose one desire was to be a small-town parish priest—actually began during my early years in the Catskills. The people to whom God entrusted the task of shaping my life during those early years are an important part of the story. All were vital to my development as a Catholic priest and an evangelist "who brings glad tidings."

My parents, Frank and Mildred Bertolucci, came from strong Italian-Catholic stock. I am their first-born son, dedicated by them to the Lord from my earliest years. I can recall the sense of awe and reverence I experienced whenever they took me to St. Patrick's Church in Catskill.

To this day visits to the Blessed Sacrament are my favorite form of devotion. From my earliest years I have had an unbroken sense of the Lord's presence in the sacrament. Even as a young boy I knew that someday I would serve God as a priest.

My father owned a small grocery store on lower Main Street in Catskill. We lived above the store for many years, later moving around the corner on Broad Street. My fondest childhood memories are of family events in that home on Broad Street.

The little grocery store was to remain a prominent feature of my childhood even after Dad sold it. I ran errands to the store almost everyday. Following my parents' instructions as I made purchases for them helped me learn the practical values of responsibility and thrift. I also learned about the spiritual principle of servanthood—an attitude I hold dear to this day.

The notions of working hard, earning one's own

living, and not hesitating to perform any task—no matter how menial—were ingrained in me from childhood. Because I was an only child for the first ten years of my life, until my brother Francis was born, I was expected to perform many different chores. This training has helped me engage in humble tasks of service. I am glad to serve in these ways because it is my way of affirming and praising those people, like my dad and mom, who have led simple, hard-working lives.

Our family never had much money, but life at home was always orderly, and we had food on the table three times a day. After selling the grocery store, Dad worked as a salesman, a clerk in a clothing store, and, later, as a janitor in a public school.

Like Dad, my mother worked hard so that our family could be provided for. Both my parents viewed their lives as the fulfillment of God's plan for them: to love each other and raise their two sons as best they knew how.

For many years we lived right next door to my father's parents, John and Josephine Bertolucci. I am named for my grandfather, but my grandparents' influence on my life extends far beyond my name. Once my grandmother sat me on her lap and spoke to me of the priesthood. She felt it her duty to encourage the formation of a priestly vocation in me, if that was what God had in mind. Her concern turned out to be prophetic.

Not far from our house was a Franciscan monastery. My grandparents were Third Order Franciscans, dedicated to Franciscan ideals of prayer and

Christian service. No wonder, as I write this, I find myself so fulfilled living in a Third Order Franciscan Monastery at the University of Steubenville in Ohio. God was preparing me for this even as a child.

My first encounter with the mystery of death happened one day after school. I came home to the news that Grandma Bertolucci had died. Our tears flowed freely in response to our loss. Even so, Grandma's wake opened a whole new world of experience. I have never forgotten that day, so full was it of powerful emotions, yet so profoundly influenced by the strong faith of family and friends. We knew the eternity to which Grandma had gone and were reminded ourselves to prepare well for death. The memory of that day has returned to me countless times, especially during the long hours I have spent in funeral parlors and at graves comforting the bereaved.

My grandmother's death was not my first encounter with great pain and loss. A few years earlier, during the height of World War II, my father was drafted. I will never forget the day he left the Catskill bus terminal. As I watched him go, feelings of fear, uncertainty, and insecurity welled up inside me. He was being taken from me, and I felt I could ill afford to lose him. My mother stood next to me, weeping. Our lives were being shaken to the roots.

For the next two years my father was someone I saw only on occasional furloughs. Those were years of fright for a small child. Added to the loss of my father were terrifying experiences of black-outs and air-raid drills. The Saturday theater matinees I attended every week always included newsreels full of the most vivid war scenes. My father wrote frequently and his letters often made Mother weep. Because we needed money she was forced to work, and I was sometimes left completely on my own at home.

Those dark events influenced my formation as a person, causing me to detest war. To this day I continually seek the mind of Christ about this human tragedy called war. I frequently intercede for peace between nations, praying that other children may be spared the awful effects of war.

For every unhappy memory of childhood, I have many wonderful memories. I fondly remember the diocesan priests who served our parish and the sisters who taught in our parish school. Today it is fashionable to be critical of the pre-Vatican II Church. But those were good years for me. My vocation to the priesthood began to take root during my years as an altar boy learning the old Latin responses to the Mass. The rituals, the always-open church, the many visits to the Blessed Sacrament, and the loving care and discipline I received were among the most valuable contributors to the fabric of my life.

The closer I got to the mysteries of life in those days, especially as an altar boy, the more secure I felt in the presence of the Holy One. That security, that sense of God's presence and power have sustained me throughout my life. It has produced in me a love for God which fills me with joy and delight.

My vocation to the priesthood took root when I

was a child, but it blossomed during the three years I served as a lay teacher in the parochial school system of the Diocese of Albany. Gradually, I became aware that I wanted to do more for my students than I was able to as a lay professional. The dream that had been stirring in me since my childhood days, gazing out my bedroom window at the mountains, came once again to the surface. I wanted to be a priest!

I arrived at the Theological College of the Catholic University of America in 1961, and from then on I knew that I had "come home," that I was doing what God wanted of me.

May 29, 1965, found me in the Cathedral of the Immaculate Conception in Albany. I was being ordained a priest of the church. At the solemn moment of prostration, as I lay on the floor of that holy sanctuary, I surrendered completely to God's plan for my life. Later, the bishop laid his hands on my head, and I was declared a priest forever. Little did I know that in a few short years another laying on of hands would cause an explosion of God's love within me.

The young man, who never dreamed of leaving the region he was raised in, was to find his feet standing on distant foreign shores, called forth from family and friends to bring glad tidings to many parts of the world. Before long, in a way I had never before imagined, I would experience the true meaning of what is written in the Acts of the Apostles: "You will receive power when the Holy Spirit comes down on you. Then you are to be my witnesses in Jerusalem, throughout Judea and Samaria, yes, even to the ends of the earth" (Acts 1:8).

The sentiments expressed in that passage started to become a reality for me during the first part of 1969, a year in which God intervened dramatically to change my life forever.

ONE

The Holy Spirit Rushes In

O NE DAY EARLY IN THE WINTER of 1969 a fellow priest came up to me and said, "John, I think something is missing in your life."

I found that remark a bit insulting because, the way I looked at it, my life could not have been better. Four years earlier I had been ordained to serve God in the priesthood, and I found priestly service rewarding and exciting. I was also in the process of getting my second graduate degree, and I was teaching my favorite courses to eager college students. I had never been happier.

Despite my self-satisfaction, I knew that my brother priest was expressing a vitality and enthusiasm in his own life that I did not have in mine. So I agreed to accept his invitation to attend a prayer meeting for priests held every Monday night. The very next Monday I was there. Rather than being offended at some strange spectacle, I was touched by the way these men, brother priests of mine, prayed

together using their own simple words spontane-
ously rather than just reading words out of a book.

They sat in a small circle, praying out loud and
reading from the Bible. Every one of them had a
Bible on his lap. I was struck that night by how
seriously these priests seemed to be taking the
scriptures.

I left that meeting impressed but untouched, or so
I thought. The next morning as I stood at the holy
table and celebrated the sacred liturgy I experienced
the presence of God as never before. He was with me
in a profound way during that Mass and I knew it.
But afterwards I forgot about the experience and
continued as if nothing extraordinary had happened.

A few weeks later, while on retreat at a monastery
in Vermont, I came across group of young lay
Catholics who were involved in prayer meetings. I
first noticed them as I looked out on the congregation one morning while celebrating Mass.

They looked different than anyone I had ever seen.
Their faces radiated great joy; they sang the hymns
enthusiastically and they raised their hands while
praying. I was especially moved by their devotion
when they received the Holy Eucharist. So intrigued
was I that I approached them after the liturgy.

"Who are you?" I asked.

"Catholic pentecostals" was their simple reply.
They then began telling me their personal stories
about how Jesus Christ had become real to them
through their involvement in the pentecostal move-
ment. No one had ever shared about their spirituality

so personally with me and I was moved.

One of the monks overheard our conversation and told me that relatives of his were also Catholic pentecostals. "In fact," he said, "they attend a weekly prayer meeting in Glenville, New York, not far from where you live." I decided right then to go to that prayer meeting and see if there was any relationship between what I had seen in these young people and what I had experienced during and after the priests' prayer meeting.

The Glenville group met on Fridays and it happened that the Friday I chose to attend was February 14. That day, Valentine's Day 1969, is a day I will never forget. On that day John Bertolucci, priest, holder of two graduate college degrees, instructor of college students, and pastoral counselor, experienced the tangible presence and love of Jesus Christ as never before.

It still amazes me how things went that day. Before I arrived at the house for the meeting, I experienced all kinds of problems. Small, almost unexplainable things went wrong all day. Some big things went wrong too. On the way to the meeting, already late, I skidded off the road in my car and had to find a farmer to pull it out of the ditch. It was as though some unseen person—or power—was trying to keep me from that prayer meeting.

When I finally arrived, I was ushered into a living room filled with people praying. I found a seat and began looking the group over. What beautiful, peaceful faces I saw! Off in one corner was a priest I did not know. He seemed to radiate the presence of God. I kept staring at him and telling myself: whatever he has, I want it!

I sat like that for a while, and then, all of a sudden, I made a request that was really uncharacteristic of me at that time.

"Please pray for me," I blurted out.

My request was answered with a chorus of "Praise God! Hallelujah!" from every corner of the room. Everyone began praying with renewed enthusiasm, and the priest came over and asked me to kneel. Without hesitation, I did so. Then he put his hands on my head, said a prayer, and, to my complete surprise and amazement, the Holy Spirit rushed into my life bringing a warmth and love and peace that I had never before experienced.

The priest prayed: "Lord, let him be at peace. Let him relax and let go, because you want to do a marvelous thing in his life." The more he prayed the more I relaxed, and the more I relaxed the more the Holy Spirit rushed in. Something marvelous certainly was happening to me.

Then the priest began praying in a language I thought was Hebrew. I assumed that he had learned that sacred language in the seminary. As I listened to him, and an urge to pray out loud came over me. I opened my mouth and, to my complete surprise, began speaking in a new language, one I had never studied. Like Peter and Paul and other Christians throughout the centuries, I had received the gift of tongues!

What a sight it must have been! Here I was, a

respectable Roman Catholic priest, kneeling in the middle of a suburban living room, praising God in an unknown tongue and crying like a baby. But whether it was a spectacle or not, no one in that room cared a bit. They were all rejoicing and so was I. I had just encountered in a new way the Lord Jesus Christ and had experienced his Holy Spirit as at Pentecost. I got to my feet a new man. Returning to my seat, all I could say was, "It's true! It's true! It's true!"

That night I returned to my apartment rather late. But I was too excited to sleep. I picked up a Bible and began reading the writings of St. Paul in the New Testament. What had always been an academic chore for me was now a thrill—I could not put that Bible down. The words simply came alive. Everything that had been written in that precious book centuries ago was now as real to me as if I was experiencing life in the apostolic church itself. I found that I was identifying with the supernatural experiences recorded in the Acts of the Apostles. The extraordinary things that Peter and Paul, Barnabas and Timothy experienced as they toiled to build Christ's church were real to me.

What I experienced that night was only the beginning of a love affair with the sacred scriptures. I have come to understand what it the church really means by speaking of the *living word of God*. That night I truly experienced the word of God, popping off those pages and into my life. I was reading the written word of God, and through it the living Word of God was dealing personally with me. I had discovered the greatest treasure in the world!

What happened to me that night? Some Christians might say I was "born again." I encountered Jesus Christ in a personal way, and I committed my life to him in a way that made my ordination as a priest even more meaningful. But it was more than that. I also had a great experience with the Holy Spirit. I received power to pray in a new language and to understand scripture in a new way. This experience is what my new pentecostal friends called "being baptized in the Holy Spirit."

What is this "baptism in the Holy Spirit?" And why did a well-adjusted, happy priest need it anyway? The dramatic conversion stories you usually hear are those of people who were addicted to drugs or alcohol or who had committed terrible crimes and were in prison. Aren't those the only kind of people who need God to do dramatic things to turn their lives around?

The baptism in the Holy Spirit, or the release of the Spirit as some of my brothers and sisters call it, is not something that God reserves for rare occasions and special cases of need. Today, millions of Catholics and Christians of many other traditions have been baptized in the Holy Spirit. Nuns, priests and bishops have been baptized in the Holy Spirit. Monks and sisters behind cloister walls have been baptized in the Holy Spirit. Men and women from all walks of life, of every race, and living on every continent on earth have been baptized in the Holy Spirit.

Why? Because it is a normal part of Christian life.

Our loving, heavenly Father intends for every one of his sons and daughters to receive the power of the Holy Spirit to live the kind of life he wants them to live. It is simply impossible for us to live that life on this earth without help from heaven. We are faced with too much temptation, too much distraction. We simply cannot do it on our own. That is why God sends his Holy Spirit into our lives. The Spirit brings with him the power to live the lives God wants us to live.

Isn't that precisely the kind of grace we receive when the Holy Spirit comes to us in the sacrament of confirmation? Don't we have a very personal contact with Jesus Christ everytime we receive the Holy Eucharist?

True, true, true. These sacraments certainly do bring us divine grace. They certainly do strengthen us to live for Jesus Christ. That is why I always tell Catholic pentecostals to take advantage of the sacraments. God works through them. Every Catholic who has been baptized in the Holy Spirit should receive the sacraments as often as possible. But everyone who receives the sacraments should also be willing to receive the baptism in the Holy Spirit because it is different. It is something more. Through it God offers a further grace of spiritual power. The baptism in the Holy Spirit involves a fuller release of the power of the Spirit, who is already part of our lives because of our reception of the other sacraments.

This is what St. Paul was getting at when he wrote to Timothy, a leader of the early church and one of the first bishops: "I remind you to stir into flame the gift of God bestowed when my hands were laid on you. The Spirit God has given us is no cowardly spirit, but rather one that makes us strong, loving, and wise."(2 Tm 1:6-7)

The experiences of those involved in the charismatic renewal, are like that. We receive the gift of the Holy Spirit when a brother or sister Christian lays hands on us and prays a simple prayer of faith to Jesus. The Spirit which we receive is indeed one who makes us strong, loving, and wise. We experience new power to live better lives, regardless of prior circumstances in our lives. We experience a hunger to pray, to read scripture, and to accept the graces Jesus gives when we receive the sacraments. All these things are, or should be, a normal part of the daily life of every Roman Catholic Christian.

The baptism in the Holy Spirit, while not a sacrament, is closely related to the sacraments because it opens up a whole new dimension of Christian experience. When a child or an adult convert receives Holy Communion for the first time, a whole new world of participation in the liturgical life of the church opens for them. The baptism in the Holy Spirit has a similar, but even more profound, effect. When we experience it, we find that we look at the world in an entirely new way. Our fondest desire is to learn more about God. We find that praying, both in private and in public—at prayer meetings and at Mass—is enjoyable. We want to be around other Christians. We want to listen to

Christian music, read Christian books, hear Christian teaching. We find that as we do these things, God blesses us more and more. He heals us of mental and physical hurts and gives us power to do good things that have seemed impossible for us before. He literally finds dozens of ways to bless and make us happy!

One thing we also find out very quickly is that the baptism in the Holy Spirit is only the beginning of this new way of life. As we discover these wonderful new blessings and abilities, we also begin to find out how weak and vulnerable we really are. We find out how much we still have to learn about being faithful sons and daughters of God. When we are tempted, we are sorely tempted. When we stumble in our walk with the Lord and commit a sin, we are painfully aware of what we have done.

The baptism in the Holy Spirit, you see, is not magic. It is very normal and natural. It does not change us completely. We are still human beings. We still have weaknesses and failures. But we also have the Spirit of God, the same Spirit who raised Jesus Christ from death to life. The same Spirit who, through the apostles and saints throughout the ages, has healed bodies and minds and worked all kinds of miracles.

This sounds dramatic. It should. Life with Jesus is supposed to be dramatic. But it is also very ordinary. We still have to get up in the morning, wash ourselves, and brush our teeth. We still eat and work and struggle to make ends meet. But we have the advantage of doing it all while enjoying an exciting relationship with Jesus Christ.

God wants every Christian adult to know Jesus Christ in a personal way, to accept him as personal Savior and Lord. God wants every Christian to appropriate the power of the Holy Spirit and to live by his holy word. This is what normal Christian living is all about. The men and women who have been baptized in the Holy Spirit and are living according to the word are only doing what is normal. They have accepted the complete grace of our faith that God intends for everyone.

All these thoughts did not occur to me that first night, of course. That night was the beginning of a special time of grace. I had just met Jesus Christ in a very intimate way. I had experienced covenant love with him, much the way, I suppose, a man and woman or special friends experience love. Just as in that human love relationship, the Lord granted me a honeymoon time, a glorious period of several months during which he taught me that I could rely on him in every way for everything I needed.

This was my initiation into what is now called the charismatic renewal. It began in 1967 when a group of Catholic students and faculty members at Duquesne University in Pittsburgh met for a retreat. These people already knew the Lord and were serving him through their involvement in the church. But they knew something was missing in their lives. While studying the scriptures concerning Pentecost, they noticed that things changed radically when the Holy Spirit came into someone's life. Divine power was released. They wanted to experience this power themselves.

The group decided to spend a day in prayer and to beseech the Lord to give this same kind of power to them. In answer to their prayers, the Lord baptized them in the Holy Spirit and gave them the gift of speaking in tongues. In a few short years charismatic prayer groups had sprung up from coast to coast and in many other countries as well. The new Pentecost was beginning to take root.

About the same time, I was happily completing my first assignment, assistant pastor of Sacred Heart Parish in Castleton-on-Hudson, New York. I was given a new assignment with a twofold purpose: I was to serve in college ministry at Maria College in Albany and as chaplain to the Motherhouse of the Sisters of Mercy. I also decided I needed more wisdom and power to minister, so I turned to psychology and began studying for yet another degree, this one in pastoral counseling.

Then came Valentine's Day, 1969, and everything changed for me. One day I was riding along on my high horse thinking I had all the answers and the next day I was back in a kind of spiritual boyhood, learning what it meant to live a full Christian life.

One of the first things I discovered was what wisdom really is. I had thought, as so many of us do, that wisdom and spiritual power come from study and hard work. But my experience with Jesus Christ and his Holy Spirit showed me that true wisdom and power can come only from God. If I want to apply real wisdom and spiritual power to a particular situation, I have to yield to the Holy Spirit. He then performs the particular work through me. In order for me to cooperate, I have to have the experience of the Holy Spirit.

After my baptism in the Holy Spirit, I had to reorient myself. My approach to ministry, particularly my approach to psychotherapy, had to change. It had to be christianized.

Now do not get me wrong. I am not trying to discredit education or psychology as a field of study. But I have learned that if I do not respect the scriptures, if I do not have a relationship with the Lord, if I do not utilize prayer in my life and ministry, I am not really ministering. If I use only human tools, I get only human results. I have to use the tools provided by the Holy Spirit if I expect to produce the kinds of results that God wants.

Oh, how I wish I had known that earlier! I thank God that he revealed this great secret to me when he did. This is why I feel compelled to proclaim the truth about Jesus Christ and the baptism in the Holy Spirit with as much vigor as possible. What has been a secret is not meant to be a secret at all! God wants everyone to have the same kind of relationship with Jesus Christ and to experience the power of the Holy Spirit in their daily lives. It is normal Christianity, intended for every person who wants to follow Jesus.

Back in 1969, I was learning these things slowly but steadily. I found that I had to let go of many things in my life after that experience with Jesus. He had different plans than mine. I knew I had to follow his plans rather than my own. The learning process was sometimes painful and I was sometimes confused. Certain people misunderstood me, and sometimes I misunderstood what the Lord was saying to me. But those months were filled with glorious experiences! Although God was weeding many things out of my life, he was very good to me. He found dozens of ways every day to show how much he loved me. I did my best to return love to him. Like I said, it was a real honeymoon.

TWO

Anointed to Preach

ON FEBRUARY 15, the day after my encounter with the Holy Spirit, two nuns came by my apartment. As their chaplain, I was attending a day-long conference with them, and they were giving me a ride. I had spent most of the night reading the New Testament. As a matter of fact, I don't remember sleeping, though I must have at least dozed off. I should have been tired. But I wasn't. Not a bit. At eight o'clock I was ready to go, expecting that God had great plans for me. I did not realize how dramatic those plans would turn out to be!

As we drove to the conference site, the two sisters in the front seat noticed the big grin that spread across my face. They kept exchanging glances, trying to decide whether they should say anything to me. Finally, the sister who was not driving turned around and asked if I was feeling all right.

"Never felt better in my life," I replied.

A little while later she turned around again, leaned over the back of her seat, and whispered, "Were you prayed over for the baptism in the Holy Spirit last night?"

"I sure was, sister," I answered, my grin getting bigger and bigger.

"I was prayed with last week," she said. "Isn't it wonderful?"

Later, at the conference, the sister who was in charge of the day's program rushed up to tell me that the main speaker, who was flying in from New York City, had been detained en route. "You'll have to fill in for him," she said.

I had come to the conference expecting only to sit and listen. I was not in the least prepared to give a major sermon during the liturgy, but I agreed to do my best.

I had never been known as a particularly good preacher, but that day I preached like I had never preached before. It was not yet twenty-four hours since the Lord had baptized me in his Holy Spirit and I was on fire with the love of God. So I preached, very simply, from my heart. And the Lord worked in the hearts of these sisters who heard me.

Afterwards, as I stood at the rear of the meeting room, I was bombarded with compliments. The sisters had really been inspired by what I had said. They were making comments like, "What has happened to you," and "If we knew you could preach like that, we would have asked you to speak in the first place."

I did not know it at the time, but that day the Lord was opening up a whole new world of ministry for me. He gave me a special grace, an anointing, to be a preacher. Within a few short years I was to preach to hundreds of thousands of people on every continent on earth. I would speak to Catholics and non-Catholics, lay people and clergy, in Jerusalem and Rome. I had been called to be an evangelist.

No matter where I spoke or to what kind of audience, I would emphasize the same message that I delivered to the sisters that morning. If you want to live a truly Christian life, if you want to be a Christ-lover and Christ-bearer, you have to have a personal experience of God's love in your life. You have to know Jesus Christ in a personal way. You have to receive the gift of his Holy Spirit.

After my experience with the sisters, I returned to the routine of my life: teaching theology, celebrating Mass, and preaching sermons. The anointing that the Lord in his goodness had given me continued. The experience of preaching without the need for any special preparation continued. As a matter of fact, I did not have to prepare a sermon, or a class, for at least six months.

When I returned to the classroom, I told my theology students to set aside all the notes they had been taking for so many months.

"We're going to start from scratch," I said. "I have been telling you about all these wonderful Christian ethics. Now I want to talk to you about Jesus Christ. We have to start with him. He is the foundation of any moral code, of any system of ethics, of any way of life that is to be called by the name of Christianity."

The students looked at me like I had flipped my lid. So I just started talking to them about Jesus in a very simple way. I explained what I had experienced and told them they could experience. Those students sensed that something was on fire inside me, but the change was too much for most of them.

It occurred to me that the students might expect me to say these things, they might even think that it was part of my job as a priest to talk about Jesus Christ. So I decided to bring in some lay men and women who had been baptized in the Spirit. After all, the example of lay men and women on fire with the love of the Lord prompted me to yield my heart and my soul to Jesus Christ. If anyone could get through to these students, it would be lay people.

I asked a couple from the Glenville prayer group to come and speak to my students. I also asked them to bring their children with them so that the students could hear about Jesus Christ, not only from a married couple, but also from young people like themselves. They did come, and in a simple way, almost childlike in its simplicity, they spoke about the Lord Jesus Christ and the power of the Holy Spirit in their lives.

Do you know what happened? By the end of that semester, one of my theology classes became a prayer group. The entire class yielded to the baptism in the Holy Spirit and became one of the first prayer groups in the Albany, New York area.

A few days after I dropped the "pentecostal bombshell" on my theology students, I had another memorable experience. I was in my apartment reading when I heard a knock at the door. It was a student from a local seminary and he had come to pour out his heart to me.

"Father John," he said, "tomorrow I am going to

leave the seminary. I am an agnostic, I no longer believe in God and I want out. I don't believe anything I'm reading and studying, and I'm tired of being a hypocrite. But I know something wonderful has happened to you and whatever it is, I want it."

I was really very moved by this young man's predicament, and I wanted to pray with him. I knew that Jesus would do something life-changing for him, just like he had for me, but I just didn't know what to do. I had never prayed with anyone the way my pentecostal friends had. I wasn't sure how to tap into the power of the Holy Spirit.

"I don't know exactly what to do," I told the seminarian. "But I'll try to do for you what the priest who prayed over me did for me. Let's see, first, you kneel down; then I put my hands here on your head; and then I will pray for you from my heart."

I had just begun to pray when the young man burst into tongues. I was so surprised that I jumped back a couple of feet. I had never seen anything happen so quickly, but I could see that the Holy Spirit was indeed at work. So I continued to pray with him. We prayed that he would recommit his life to the Lord and be filled with the Holy Spirit. After a while he left, an agnostic no longer.

The next morning a seminary faculty member called me up and said, "What are you doing up there? The young man who came to see you last night is back here at the seminary, and he is so turned on about God I'm wondering about his sanity." However, before long other seminarians came to talk and pray with me.

What a remarkable experience that was for me as a priest. I was supposed to help people with their spiritual problems. I was supposed to comfort them and show them how God could help them. But this time, instead of relying on the wisdom of psychotherapy, I relied upon prayer. I prayed a very simple prayer, and this humble young man turned his heart to Jesus Christ, who was able to do for him in a few moments what I probably would have been unable to do in months or even years of counseling. In the twinkling of an eye the God of heaven had revealed himself, in all his glory and power, to one of his beloved children. In seconds he put to rest the confusion and turmoil that had been developing for years in this young mind. I have seen that happen literally hundreds of times since that night.

My psychological training taught me one very valuable lesson about the importance of listening to people. I had two wonderful psychology teachers: Brother John Egan of Iona College in New York and Father Charles Curran of the University of Chicago. Both taught me an appreciation for the admonition found in the Epistle of St. James: "Be quick to hear, slow to speak, slow to anger" (Jas 1:9). The simple wisdom of that verse and the example of these men led me to appreciate the value of listening to people and then praying for their needs.

Most people today think of me as an evangelistic preacher. But I am also a counselor. I spend a great deal of time, when I am not on the road preaching, counseling students at the Franciscan University of Steubenville where I am a faculty member. The most incredible things happen during those counseling sessions. The same kind of evangelistic fervor that motivates me when I am preaching to a crowd motivates me when I am counseling one-to-one.

When I am on a stage preaching, my goal is to lead people to a life-changing encounter with Jesus Christ. That is the same goal I have in every counseling session. When I listen, I listen closely, and, as a result, people pour out their hearts to me. Once this happens I can get to the root of the problem, and we can pray that the Lord will heal them. In every situation I have found that either the emotional or spiritual health of the person I am counseling improves when I listen and I pray.

Once, as I was preparing to address a large crowd at an evangelistic gathering, I was asked to spend a few minutes with a woman who had tried three times to commit suicide. She was so determined to kill herself that she had been committed to the mental care ward at a nearby hospital. Her doctors had tried everything but were unable to help her, so they agreed to let some friends take her to see me.

I met her in a small room near the auditorium where I was to speak. I knew that she was married and had four teenage children. Her husband was waiting outside the room, pacing nervously in the hall. The woman just sat there, bandages on both wrists where she had cut them with razor blades.

"What's going on here, honey?" I asked her. "I understand you have four children."

"Yes, I do," she said. "I love them and they love me."

"Honey," I said, "you have tried to slit your wrists three times; they've had to lock you up in a mental ward; what's going on in your life that's so terrible?"

She looked at me, sensed that I really wanted to help her, and poured out her story in a torrent of anguish.

"I have been married a long time," she said. "I have loved my husband more than anything else. He has been everything to me. I have worked hard to make our house beautiful for him to enjoy. I've struggled to raise the children well so he would be proud of them. I've given him everything. And then I caught him in adultery. After everything I have done for him, he went to another woman."

Well, my heart went out to her. I touched her very gently and whispered in her ear the only words that could do anything for her: "Your mistake, honey, was in making your husband the lord of your life. There can only be one lord in your life and that has to be the Lord Jesus Christ.

"You know something, he understands just how you feel because he, too, was betrayed by someone he loved. Did you know that Jesus loved Judas? He spent three years with Judas. They shared many things together. And Judas betrayed him. Of all the painful things Jesus suffered in his life, that must have been among the worst."

She looked into my eyes, and I continued: "Right now you need to turn to Jesus. Tell him you are sorry for neglecting him and trying to take your own life. He will forgive you and he will come into your heart and comfort you. He will also help you forgive your husband. The psychiatrists can only do so much. Jesus Christ is the only one who can bring the deep healing you need."

She took me at my word. So I asked her to kneel down on the floor, and I heard her confession. Then I placed my hands on her head and led her in a prayer of humility: "Lord Jesus, Son of God, set me free; I invite you into my life; give me from your cross the grace of forgiveness. Let the power of your Holy Spirit come upon me, that I may with your love love the one who has hurt me."

After we prayed that prayer, she began to sob, then to weep. I knew that the Lord was touching her. The dam had broken within her, and all the garbage was flowing out. Jesus Christ is the greatest garbage collector in the world. He has cleaned so much junk out of so many lives, it boggles the mind just to think of what he has done.

Next, I got on the intercom and asked the people who were helping me to send in the husband. He was a big, burly fellow. He came into the room looking scared to death. Like so many of us, he looked tough on the outside but inside he was more like a little child.

He couldn't do much of anything but look at his wife who was still kneeling there on the floor, tears rolling down her cheeks.

"Honey," I said to the wife, "you look him straight in the eyes and just tell him what's going on inside you."

She looked up at him and said what are probably the two most healing sentences that anybody could ever hear: "I forgive you. And I love you."

I knelt there and watched as this great big fellow just melted in front of his wife. He came crashing to his knees and he said, "Father John, I don't know what you've done, but whatever you've done for her, I want you to do for me."

Well, anybody who knows me knows that I don't need much more invitation than that. I was ready to go.

So I instructed him, told him to ask for forgiveness, and then prayed with him. The Lord repeated the miracle again. He cleansed that man of his sin, cleaned the garbage out of his life, and baptized him in the Holy Spirit.

Let me tell you, there is nothing more dramatic than a great big football-player type kneeling on the floor, tears streaming down his face, praying in tongues.

God healed those two people. He healed their marriage. He set them free to start over again without bitterness, without enmity, filled with the joy and peace of the Holy Spirit.

He is ready now to do the same for anyone. God heals the deepest hurts, if we will allow him to. No problem is insurmountable for God. "Receive the Holy Spirit," Jesus said in Luke 18:37. "If you forgive men's sins, they are forgiven them." This scripture, on one level, is the foundation for the sacrament of reconciliation. But on another level it applies to every one of us who are also his disciples. We have the power to forgive someone else. That woman used the power the Lord gave her. She let go of her hurt, and she forgave the one who had hurt her. That act of forgiveness opened his heart to repent of his sin, to seek Jesus as Lord of his life, to receive the Holy Spirit and begin to live a new life.

If there is anyone in your life whom you have not forgiven, do it now. Turn to the Lord in prayer and tell him you forgive that person. I know it is hard, but he will help you let go if you really want to! Don't let unforgiveness dwell in your heart. It will only grow into worse demons and will be harder to get rid of later. Let it go. Give it to Jesus. He's ready to collect any garbage you have right now.

While you're at it, if you have not surrendered your life to Jesus, if you have not invited him to be your personal Lord, to rule over your mind and heart and spirit, do it, right now. Put down the book, turn to Jesus in a very humble, personal prayer. Here are some words to help you:

> Lord Jesus Christ, Son of the Living God, I know that you came into the world to die on the cross and save me from my sins. I want to change my life. I want to commit my heart and soul and mind to you. I invite you into my life right now. I want you to be my personal Savior, the Lord of my life. Come, Lord Jesus, into my heart. Clean the garbage out of my life. Fill me with your Holy Spirit. Wash me clean and turn my life around so I can live for you.

After you have prayed this prayer, you may begin to feel different about yourself and about your relationship to the Lord. Then again, you may not. If you do feel different, I want you to begin immediately to build a personal daily prayer life and to form a daily habit of Bible reading. I will say more about this later.

If you feel no immediate change, continue to pray that prayer, at least once every day, until you do experience something. God is eager to initiate personal contact with you. When he does, you will know it. So, pray that prayer devoutly and patiently and God will speak to you.

I know that God will deal with you after you pray humbly to him because he has done so in my life. He has done so in the lives of literally thousands of people whom I have had the privilege of leading in a similar kind of prayer.

THREE

Living Each Day in the Spirit

T HE EXPERIENCE I HAD with the couple who had been torn apart by adultery is an example of the way the priestly ministry is supposed to work all the time. Ministers of the gospel are supposed to help people get in touch with Jesus Christ. He is the only one who can give eternal help to people's problems, the only one who can show people how to live, and the only one who can forgive, heal, restore, and sustain anyone who comes to him, anytime and with any need.

One Bible passage that is full of meaning for me as a priest, as someone responsible for the spiritual welfare of others, is from 1 Peter 5:

> To the elders among you I, a fellow elder, a witness of Christ's sufferings and sharer in the glory that is to be revealed, make this appeal. God's flock is in your midst; give it a shepherd's care. Watch over it willingly as God would have

you do, not under constraint; and not for shameful profit either, but generously. Be examples to the flock, not lording it over those assigned to you, so that when the chief Shepherd appears you will win for yourselves the unfading crown of glory. (1 Pt 5:1-4)

I read this passage before my Valentine's Day experience, but it had never meant much to me. After that great day, when the Lord favored me with the baptism of his Holy Spirit, this passage came alive for me. I began to see ministry in a whole new way. I was anxious to tend the flock the Lord had entrusted to me and anxious to use all the gifts he had given me. I wanted to bring everyone to the same kind of encounter with Jesus Christ. I wanted everyone to find the abundance of life that the good Lord has to offer.

At the same time I was also learning in very practical ways that the baptism in the Holy Spirit was not a one-shot experience but truly the initiation into a new way of life. I had to learn more about the Spirit-filled life and I had to learn to rely on the Lord to care for my needs. The passage in the first letter of Peter continues:

You younger men must be obedient to your elders. In your relations with one another clothe yourselves with humility, because God "is stern with the arrogant but to the humble he shows kindness." Bow humbly under God's mighty

hand, so that in due time he may lift you high. Cast all your cares on him because he cares for you.
(1 Pt 5:5-7)

If there is ever a moment that I am moved to take scripture literally and to believe that every word is eternal, ageless truth, it is when I read passages like this. God's word is telling us that when we humble ourselves and follow his plan for our lives, rather than our own he "lifts us high." More than that, we can cast every care, every burden, every need, every anxiety on him, because he cares about us. He will take care of us and will never let us down. No prayer we pray will ever go unanswered. No real need we have will ever go unmet.

I learned these truths when I had some interesting experiences those first few weeks after I was baptized in the Holy Spirit.

One day when I went to the post office to mail a package. I learned how God cares for even the small things in my life. The clerk weighed the package and told me it would cost fifty cents to mail. I reached in my pocket to get the money, but there was nothing there. I didn'teven have a penny. What a predicament!

My pentecostal friends had been telling me to ask God for everything. So right away my newly discovered spiritual self said, "Why don't you ask the Lord for the fifty cents." The other half of me, still studying psychology in graduate school, replied, "Come on, John, be reasonable. If you want the money, you have to walk back to your apartment and get the fifty cents."

It was a real spiritual tug of war. My spiritual side said, "This is a test! Step out in faith and ask God for the fifty cents." But the other side countered, "Here you are, a theologian. You know better than to go to God with a simple request like that. Salvation of the world, yes. Healing of all human problems, yes. But fifty cents? You can take care of that yourself."

I am happy to report that my guardian angel won that tug of war. I swallowed my pride, my sophistication, my theological expertise, and I prayed, "Father, in Jesus' name, I need fifty cents!" After praying like that, quietly but sincerely, in the lobby of the U.S. post office, I decided that I had to walk back to my apartment, my package still unmailed.

I stepped out of the post office, and a car pulled up in front of me. A nun I knew was driving it, and she hollered, "Father John, how are you."

"Hi, sister," I replied.

"Where are you going?" she asked.

"I have to get fifty cents to mail a package."

"I have two quarters right here on the dashboard," she answered. "Why don't you take them so you don't have to go all the way home."

This experience showed me that I could come to my Father for anything. The Lord wants to help me deal with life just like a human father wants to help his own son. When I need something, he's there to give it to me. He uses very ordinary circumstances, of course. My fifty cents came from a nun, not an angel flying down from heaven. But God was at work there, just as he is at work every day, twenty-four hours a day, taking care of the needs of those who follow the way of Jesus Christ!

A little while later I embarked on my first "pentecostal vacation," a trip to Florida with five seminarians. We planned to do some evangelistic work and to enjoy some relaxation, some fun in the sun, at the same time. We packed up the car, hopped in, and took off for Florida.

After driving for several hours, we were all getting hungry, so we began to pray about where we should eat. Ordinarily, when you are driving and you get hungry you stop at the next place you come to. But all six of us had recently encountered Jesus Christ, and we were still in our "honeymoon stage." So we asked the Lord where he wanted us to eat.

"Father, where do you want us to stop?" I prayed. "Where do you want us to be present. We know you have a plan for us, and we want to eat at the place you have planned."

We drove along praying like that, and then we decided to pull over at a gas station. We stopped the car and a man walked over, looked at us, and said, "You guys look hungry. There's a fried chicken place about two miles up the road." So we thanked him and started driving again. Up the road a little way we came to an intersection, and we realized that the man had not told us which way to turn. So we stopped again and prayed, "Lord which way do you want us to go?"

I had never done anything like this before in my life. But that night this seemed to be the way the

Lord himself wanted us to proceed. After we prayed, the consensus of the group was to turn left. We turned and drove down the road praising God to beat the band. But we saw no sign of a restaurant. All we could see at the next intersection was an Assembly of God Church. Evidently something was going on inside that church.

I knew that the Assembly of God was one of the traditional pentecostal churches, and I commanded, "Stop the car. The Lord is calling us to fellowship."

We pulled up and got out, five Catholic seminarians and a Catholic priest walking toward an Assembly of God Church. Inside a lot of singing and praying was going on. As we approached the church we realized that there was a fried chicken restaurant right behind it. After some deliberation, we changed our course, deciding that the Lord was indeed sending us to the restaurant.

Still, I knew that there was a message in this. God was telling us that wherever there are praising, praying people, he is taking care of his own. The fires of divine love are lit all over the place, even in churches that differ from ours. The Lord taught me something about ecumenism that was later to affect my ministry to a significant degree.

We got to the door of the fried chicken place and the manager met us with the news that he was closing up for the night.

"But we're hungry," I said to him.

"Well, we're closed," he answered. "But let me check in back. We may have something left."

A few minutes later he came back and said, "I have

six pieces of chicken and some other leftovers. You are welcome to them."

There were six pieces of chicken, as well as an abundant supply of mashed potatoes and coleslaw, and six hungry men to eat it all! God had provided for our needs once again. In the process, he taught me another lesson about how he takes care of all who rely on him.

Remember the story in Matthew's gospel about the lilies of the field? They don't even do any work, Jesus said. They just sit there on top of the soil and grow into beautiful flowers. God gives them everything they need. He is delighted with their growth and their beauty, the work of his own hands.

Don't you think, Jesus asked them, that if God will do so much for mere flowers, he will do much more for you, his beloved children?

Of course he will! God wants to give us everything we need to survive in this world. He wants to provide for more than just our basic needs. He also wants to give us his Holy Spirit. All these things help us grow. They help us thrive as sons and daughters of the living God. If God cares so much about the flowers of the field, blooming in glory one day and wilted the next, fit only to be thrown on the fire, how much more does he care for us. We are his beloved children, created in his image and likeness, to be treasured for all eternity! Jesus sums it up by saying: "Seek first his kingship over you, his way of holiness, and all these things will be given you besides" (see Mt 7:26-34).

Jesus wasn't speaking to children. The crowd was

full of grown men and women. Peter, James, John, and the other apostles were probably there too. They were strong men, accustomed to working hard for their daily bread. But Jesus called them little children. He challenged them to learn to rely on their own heavenly Father, just as human children rely on their human parents for food, shelter, clothing, security, and the other necessities of life.

Later, he reminded them that no matter how much human fathers and mothers might want to give good things to their children, the heavenly Father, will give much more to anyone who turns to him and humbly seeks to be his obedient son or daughter:

> So I say to you, "Ask and you shall receive; seek and you shall find; knock and it shall be opened to you."
>
> For whoever asks, receives; whoever seeks, finds; whoever knocks, is admitted. What father among you will give his son a snake if he asks for a fish, or hand him a scorpion if he asks for an egg? If you, with all your sins, know how to give your children good things, how much more will the heavenly Father give the Holy Spirit to those who ask him. (Lk 11:9-13)

Jesus isn't just speaking about food and drink. Of course, our Father is interested in giving us these good things we need to survive. He doesn't want his children to be hungry, homeless, or cold. But he wants so much more for us. He wants us to be filled with the Holy Spirit so that we can obey him and follow him to eternal life.

Without the activity of the Holy Spirit in our lives, we are lost. We cannot achieve eternal life on our own. We need Jesus Christ to be Lord of our lives every day, and we need his Holy Spirit, the one who teaches us how to live for Jesus. He is the one who brings us the power to be victorious over sin, the one who enables us to obey the commands of God. We need him even more than we need food, clothing and shelter. Survival on this earth is important, but eternal life is so much more important. We should never forget about eternity. It is a very long time compared with seventy or eighty years on earth! If we expect to get to heaven, to "win the crown" as St. Paul called it, we need the power of the Holy Spirit acting in our lives every day.

These were the kinds of lessons I was learning day by day back in 1969 after my own experience of Jesus' Holy Spirit. And these are the things I have preached about ever since. Christians must be filled with the power of the Holy Spirit if they are to obey God, receive his blessings, and eternal life. There is simply no other way. Jesus is the only way to the Father, and the only way we can be faithful to Jesus is by relying on the power of the Holy Spirit.

Pray today that Jesus will send you his Spirit. If you pray a simple prayer, humbly and sincerely, Jesus will answer it. In addition to praying, I recommend that you look up the location of the nearest charismatic prayer group (you can find one almost anywhere). Ask them when the next Life in the Spirit Seminar will be held. These seminars have been the vehicle through which millions of people— Catholics, Protestants, and people without faith— have come to meet Jesus Christ in a personal way, to be baptized in the Holy Spirit. The seminars are presented by prayer groups all over the country. If you have not received the Holy Spirit in your life, go find a prayer group and ask to take a seminar. Even if you have received the Holy Spirit, I still recommend that you attend one. You need teaching and fellowship, and the seminars are the best place I know of to receive it.

God has done many extraordinary things in my life, and he will do the same for you. He has not dealt with me as he has because I am unusually gifted or holy or worthy. I am only an ordinary priest. I am well aware of human frailty and sin. God has done what he has because he loves me and because he wants me to extend his love, his gospel to as many people as possible during my life on earth. He wants you to do the same. You may be an ordinary man or woman, but God wants to give you his Holy Spirit and to do extraordinary things in your life! Why? Because he loves you and also because he wants to reach into the lives of your family, friends, and anyone else he places in your path.

The experiences I have been recounting are, as I said earlier, ordinary Christian experiences. God wants you to have them. Ask him for them. Be confident as you ask—God will do great things in your life!

FOUR

A Spirit of Power

NOT LONG AFTER THESE FIRST experiences of living and serving as a priest under the Lordship of Jesus Christ and with the power of the Holy Spirit, I experienced the Lord speaking very explicitly about what he wanted me to do. I clearly heard him saying:

John, you have discovered new life; I have anointed you; I am giving you a very simple faith; I want you to go forth and share these things with others. I want you to make yourself available to preach the gospel whenever and wherever I call you.

After I realized exactly what the Lord wanted of me, a whole new involvement in ministry began. The first thing I knew, I was on my way to South America. I had many experiences on that trip, but the one that was most significant for me was learning about the Lord who is healer. Here is how it happened.

One day a woman came to me and told me that she had been harboring hatred in her heart for a clergyman who had hurt her very deeply five or six years before. Her hatred was literally making her sick. She was having migraine headaches, high blood pressure, ulcers, and other difficulties. She was absolutely miserable, and no doctor could do a thing for her.

By this time I had finished my graduate work in counseling and I knew what the books said I could do for her by means of psychotherapy. However, I just knew that this was not what the Lord wanted me to do. I wasn't going to be in South Amercia long enough to counsel her, and counseling may or may not have worked anyway. I placed my hands on her head and asked the Lord to deliver her from her hatred, her resentment, her bitterness. In only a few minutes the Lord accomplished in her heart what it would have taken me hours of counseling to do. She was healed in her soul and almost immediately the symptoms of disease began to disappear as well.

I remember that incident to this day because it was the first time that I began to recognize the power of God to heal. I began to see that not only does God want to free us from our sin, not only does he want to give us the good things we need, but he also wants to heal our emotions and our physical symptoms. All it takes on our part is the willingness to forgive and the willingness to turn to the Lord in faith. He will do the rest. I don't want to oversimplify matters. Divine healing is an area in which great care must be shown. I simply want to say that I believe God heals.

I have seen him do it. I have experienced it. I know that it is part of his plan for his people. I don't mean to imply, either, that all physical ailments have emotional causes. They don't.

I finished my tour of ministry in South America and returned to Albany, New York, where I was serving as vice-chancellor, a member of the bishop's staff. Each day I grew in my awareness of the magnitude of what God was doing among his people through this outpouring of the Holy Spirit in the charismatic renewal. I began to see how far and wide was this mighty work God was doing among thousands of my Catholic brothers and sisters and among members of almost every Protestant denomination.

This knowledge of God's activity among Protestants helped me get rid of any prejudice I had against them. Just as many other Catholics, I was prejudiced, particularly against those whose church services had always seemed so emotional to me. "Holy rollers" we sometimes called them. But the Lord healed me of that prejudice.

He began that healing the evening I saw the brothers and sisters in that Assembly of God Church praying and praising God. He completed it one day at a national charismatic renewal conference at the University of Notre Dame. The power of God had come over that assembly, and several men who were speaking there, called us to repent for our prejudices against Christian brothers and sisters whose beliefs and forms of worship differed from our own.

That day a man from a Protestant charismatic

group in Fort Lauderdale, Florida, was present. I found myself getting up off my knees and walking over to him, hugging him and asking his forgiveness because I had not really fully believed that God could be active among people in other churches.

I know now that God is doing mighty things among people in a host of churches. More than that, he is bringing us together. He is filling all flesh with his Holy Spirit, and one of the fruits of this outpouring of the Spirit is a desire and an ability to seek Christian unity on a very personal, grass roots level. Our progress has been slow, but it is progress nonetheless. It begins with the healing of prejudices.

Later I attended a Logos Conference on the Holy Spirit in Jerusalem. Several dozen denominations were represented, and I remember the power that came over that assembly. God healed so many of us of prejudices, and he showed us how we could serve one another and enjoy one another as brothers and sisters in Christ.

At that conference I had a brief encounter with the famous faith healer Kathryn Kuhlman. It had taken me a while to believe that God could use a woman like her to minister to people. She was quite controversial and her style was hard for many Catholics to accept. But I found out that God did indeed use her.

I attended her service at that Jerusalem conference. As I listened to her talk about healing, I tried to find something wrong with me so I, too, could be prayed with. I really wanted to go up and have her pray over me, but I couldn't find anything wrong. I wasn't sick and had not the slightest ache or pain. Unfortunately, I didn't think of my glasses. I could have had her pray for my eyesight, but it didn't occur to me.

I sat there watching others being prayed with and claiming healings. All of a sudden she stopped her healing service and said: "I want every Roman Catholic priest and Protestant minister in this room to come up here."

I was so excited that I jumped over two rows of chairs and rushed up to the stage. Miss Kuhlman prayed over me, and I was immediately overcome by the power of God. The Lord touched me through the prayer of this holy woman.

Later that night, after we had returned to our hotel, I was too excited to go up to my room. Miss Kuhlman's prayer had filled me with the power and the presence of God. So I looked into the bar and saw six Irish soldiers sitting there. These men were in Jerusalem, on leave from their peacekeeping duties along the border of Israel and Egypt.

I decided that the Lord wanted me to be bold, so I walked into the bar and shouted: "I am a priest. Get out of this bar!"

Amazingly, they obeyed. I guess that Irish soldiers far from home will usually obey a priest, at least they did that night.

I led them into another room and said, "Sit down, fellows, I have something to tell you."

I spent the next half hour talking to them about Jesus and about how they had to hand their lives over to him. I told them about the conference I was attending, and I said, "Here you are wasting your time on alcoholic spirits while there is another Spirit, the Holy Spirit, who wants to take over your lives."

Well, these poor guys just sat there, kind of scared, not really knowing what to do. I don't suppose they had ever heard a priest talk like that before.

Then, one of them said, "Father, can I go to confession?"

"You sure can," I said.

So I took him into another room and heard his confession. Then I told him I was going to lay my hands on him and pray that the Lord would come into his life. As I prayed, he fell on the floor, overcome with the Holy Spirit just as I had been a few hours earlier. After a while he got up, tears streaming down his face, full of the peace and joy of Jesus Christ and the Holy Spirit.

I didn't know it at the time but this man was the commanding officer of that group of soldiers. His men all wanted to follow his example. One at a time, another priest and I heard their confessions and prayed with them. It was simply a wonderful experience to watch the Lord work in the lives of these soldiers. It was truly a time when the Prince of Peace himself came and cared for these men who were trying so hard to keep peace in the Middle East.

I returned home from that conference with another priest from Albany. We were certain that within a few months God was going to do some dramatic and powerful things through our ministry. At the time we were leading a group of about 600 Catholics and Protestants who came together every Sunday night to pray and seek the word of the Lord. During the week, many of the Catholics from that group attended a Mass for charismatics, and I was usually the celebrant.

One evening, about two months after the Jerusalem conference, we were finishing up the liturgy and my colleague turned to me and said, "John, I feel something very powerful here. Remember when Kathryn prayed for us? I think the Lord wants us to pray for the people here, just like that."

"Brother," I said, "you've got to be kidding. Do that here? In church? Right after Mass? What if somebody comes walking in? What if the bishop finds out? It could be very embarrassing."

Well, my objections were short-lived because I knew he was right. Kathryn Kuhlman had prayed that the same power that we experienced at her service would become evident in our ministries back home. She had prophesied that this would happen. This very night God was telling us that it was time.

"O.K.," I said. "Here goes."

We asked everyone who was willing to be prayed with to line up, just like they had for communion. One-by-one we prayed with them. We placed our hands on their heads and prayed that the Holy Spirit would anoint them with power in their own lives. Crash! One after another they fell over, simply overwhelmed by the power and love of the Holy

Spirit. It was really something to see. Within a few minutes there were bodies lying all over the sanctuary.

"Resting in the Spirit" can be a powerful experience for people, but such happenings can also be abused. There is much more to the Christian life than such spiritual phenomena. My altar calls are not always that dramatic. Yet, I have come to see the value of eliciting a response from people whenever I preach. It is written: "Faith . . . comes through hearing and what is heard is the word of Christ" (Rom 10:17).

I now believe people need to take a conscious, deliberate, expressed stand for Christ. People need Jesus in their lives. When I speak to a large gathering or a small one, I usually extend an invitation at the end to everyone who has not had the incomparable privilege of accepting Christ into their heart. I ask them to think about doing it at that moment. I invite them to come forward and to permit those of us ministering to pray with them that Jesus, the Lord of Life, might come into their lives. One scripture passage I like to use on such occasions comes from the book of Revelation: "Here I stand, knocking at the door. If anyone hears me calling and opens the door, I will enter his house and have supper with him and he with me."

That is what Jesus wants to do in every life! He wants to come with supernatural, eternal power to have fellowship with us mortal humans. He wants to have supper with us! He wants to converse with us! He wants to set us free; to give us his Holy Spirit that we might live no longer for ourselves but for him!

As I said earlier, I was vice-chancellor of the Diocese of Albany, and that dramatic church service our prayer group had held was being talked about all over town. As phone calls about it came into the bishop's office during the next few days, they were sent to me. When people heard from someone at the bishop's office that things were all right, they felt reassured. Although the incident was unusual and widely talked about, there were no significant repercussions.

Some people had raised questions when I was first appointed to the bishop's staff. They asked the bishop if he really wanted a tongues-speaking charismatic on his staff. I am fortunate to have had a bishop who was truly open to the Holy Spirit. He answered their objections by saying, "I don't care if he prays standing on his head, as long as he prays." So, a little thing like a few hundred people crashing to the floor in a church after a liturgy caused hardly a ripple among the folks at the chancery.

Another thing that the Lord taught me at that time was the importance of praying for the shepherds of the church. The Lord has led me to pray every day for my bishop, for the Holy Father, and for the other shepherds he has put over me. I urge every Christian to make a similar commitment. It is easy to criticize our leaders, to see their failings, and to wish that they would do more for us. But have we prayed for them? We should pray that the Lord who called them to service in his church would fill them with the Holy Spirit. We have no business thinking about the failings of our leaders unless we are willing to pray that God will bless them.

What is the fruit of such prayer? For one thing, I have received a series of green lights in my ministry as a charismatic, preaching priest. My bishops have always supported me and encouraged me. Of course I would pray for them even if they didn't. Because they know that I support them with my prayer and my loyalty, they feel comfortable supporting me. They understand why I must do what God has called me to do.

One time I decided that I wanted to pray more directly for my bishop. But I didn't think it was the right time to ask him if I could pray over him, so I decided to look for an opportunity to pray over his office.

My chance came one day when three other charismatic priests were visiting the chancery while the bishop was out of town. So, I said to my brother priests:

"The bishop is out of town, and his secretary is out of the office. Let's go into the bishop's office and 'pray up the room.'"

They enthusiastically agreed, and we entered into the bishop's office and "prayed up the room." There we were, four priests, walking around the room praising God, praying in tongues, interceding for our shepherd, laying hands on his chair. All of a sudden, out of the corner of my eye, I saw the door open. The bishop's secretary stuck his head in. I had thought he was out of the office, but I was mistaken. Embarrassed as I could be, I quickly stopped praying and began acting like I was conducting a tour of the bishop's office:

"And over in this corner we have a painting of. . . ."

"What are you doing," the secretary asked me.

"Oh, I'm just showing them around the office here."

Now, of course, that was a lie. I was trying to cover myself like people caught in embarrassing situations sometimes do. My efforts were really silly because there is absolutely nothing wrong with praying for the bishop. It might have been a bit unorthodox. I'm pretty sure that no one had ever done it quite like that before. But it was actually a good thing to do.

Anyway, the group I was with quickly left the bishop's office, and one of the other priests suggested that the four of us celebrate mass together. "But, first," he said, "I'd like you to hear my confession, John." So we went upstairs and began praying. Suddenly it came to me.

"I can't hear your confession. I have sinned. I just told a lie. I have to go downstairs and tell Father Tom what we were really doing in that office."

So I did. I went to his office, sat down in front of his desk, and said:

"Father Tom, I have to ask your forgiveness."

"Why?" he said." "What did you do?"

"I lied to you about what we were doing in the bishop's office, that's what I did."

"Well what were you doing in there?"

"We were praying," I answered.

"Well, thank God somebody around here is praying," he replied.

That incident taught me several important lessons. They are lessons that every Christian should
learn. It is all right to admit a mistake. It is all right to
ask a brother or a sister to forgive us when we've
sinned. In fact, Jesus demands that we do. "Remove
the plank [of sin] from your own eye," Jesus said
during the Sermon on the Mount, then you will be
able to see clearly enough "to take the speck from
your brother's eye" (Mt 7:5).

Earlier in that same discourse he said: "If you
bring your gift to the altar and there recall that your
brother has anything against you, leave your gift at
the altar, go first to be reconciled with your brother,
and then come and offer your gift" (Mt 5:24).

I thank God that he has taught me this lesson. It
sounds like a hard thing to do. You must swallow
your pride, humble yourself, admit your mistake.
But almost everytime you do it, you will get a
positive reaction.

That is another lesson that Christians have to
learn: it is all right to admit that we pray. It is all right
to pray in places other than a church building or our
own home. We should be people of prayer, people
who are not ashamed to be seen turning to the Lord
in prayer. If we know that God hears our prayer, then
we should pray, loud and clear, at every opportunity.

In one of his epistles St. Paul wrote: "Rejoice
always, never cease praying, render constant thanks;
such is God's will for you in Christ Jesus" (See
2 Thes 16-18).

This is our call: to pray all the time; to render

thanks all the time. Why? Because human beings need to be in constant touch with God. We need to be turning to him throughout the day with our petitions and with thanksgiving for his ongoing care for us. This doesn't mean that we have to say formal prayers all the time. There are times and places when formal prayers like the liturgy are most important. Even so, the rest of our prayer life should consist of informal, spontaneous, from-the-heart conversation with God.

Tell God you love him; tell him you want to serve him; tell him what you are doing and how you are feeling and what you are happy about and what you would like him to do for you. It is really very easy to pray like that. All you have to do is to remember to do it!

What happens to us when we make it a habit to converse with God during the day? We are filled with joy! We experience the power and the presence of God! There is nothing like it in the whole world!

At the same time that I was learning all these other lessons, I learned in a very dramatic way the joy that comes from leading others to Jesus Christ. As a priest I had performed a number of baptisms, including baptisms of adults. So I knew what it was like to welcome a new member into the fellowship of the church. Those were always occasions of joy for me. I truly celebrated the sacraments with the new members of the church.

Even so, being able to lead people to the freedom and joy of surrendering to Jesus Christ as personal Lord and Savior is something else again. I never tire of it! It is the greatest thing in the world! I am constantly on the lookout for opportunities to pray for people to experience the kingship of Jesus in their lives and the great gift of the baptism in the Holy Spirit.

I discovered this joy in greater depth when I took a few days off to attend an ecumenical retreat. I went away for a week to a Franciscan monastery with an Assembly of God minister and an Episcopal priest. We spent our week praying together and talking about all the different ways that members of the Body of Christ had been evangelizing people down through the centuries. We also spent time comparing various techniques that we had used to lead people to Christ.

At night we removed our clerical garb, put on sports clothes, and went out at a resort area near the monastery. We proceeded to share the Good News of Jesus Christ with the people passing by. This was completely new for me. In the past, people had come to me to ask about my experience with Christ. Now I was in a public place looking for opportunities to share about Jesus with total strangers.

We used a very direct approach. We walked up to someone standing alone, especially the young street people who looked like they needed help, and we said: "Can I tell you about Jesus?"

We met with mixed reactions. Some people just walked away, but others wanted to hear what we had to say. One young man who decided to listen to what I had to say provided us not only with an exciting opportunity to evangelize but also with a chance for clergymen of different denominations to work together for the sake of the gospel. Here is how it happened.

We were walking along the boardwalk one night approaching people with our offer to talk about Jesus. This particular young man accepted and, after making sure that I was really a Catholic, admitted to me that he was what we then called a "fallen-away Catholic."

So the other two clergymen backed off a bit and gave me the chance to speak with him. One of them whispered to me, "He's one of yours; go after him." And I did. While the other two prayed, I said, "let's just walk along here and talk about Jesus Christ." As we were walking we came to a coffee house and I invited him inside for a cup of coffee. The other two ministers followed us in. To my surprise, and before we even had a chance to sit down, the owner of the place came up and introduced himself. "I'm Reverend Smith," he said. "I'm a Southern Baptist minister."

The two of us sat down, and I told the young man what Jesus Christ had done for me and encouraged him to open his life to the Lord. I told him that I would be happy to hear his confession and pray with him if he wanted me to. He decided that this was indeed what he wanted.

What happened that night was simply extraordinary. By two o'clock in the morning this fallen-away Roman Catholic had made his confession and had received Jesus Christ into his life as Lord and Savior; he had been counseled about the Christian life by the Southern Baptist minister; he had been prayed over by the Assembly of God minister for the baptism in the Holy Spirit; and he was given additional encouragement and counseling by the Episcopal priest.

What a remarkable experience that was. Four clergymen from four very different denominations working together and seeing, before our very eyes, the salvation of our God at work in a human life.

I walked home that night exclaiming: "this is what it's all about. This is real ecumenism!"

As wonderful as this experience was, it turned out to be only the beginning of a continuous experience of personal evangelism for me.

FIVE

Personal Evangelism

D URING THE FIRST FEW YEARS after my baptism in the Holy Spirit, I came to realize that every-thing that happens to me is part of God's plan. I really mean it when I say everything, even the painful and annoying aspects of life. When we are in Christ Jesus, and are doing our best to live according to his plan for our lives, everything that happens has a purpose, a glorious purpose.

I have learned, for example, that God can use occurrences that annoy me for his marvelous pur-poses. I used to be greatly annoyed whenever I missed an airplane flight. After coming to know Jesus personally and being set afire with zeal for bring others to Jesus, I have come to handle this kind of situation very differently. Everytime I have missed a plane in the last fifteen years, I have had the opportunity to witness to someone who desperately needed to come to a saving relationship with the Lord.

One time I was on my way to Dayton, Ohio, for a speaking engagement. The travel plan called for a direct flight to Dayton, but somehow I missed the plane. So the airline put me on a flight to Chicago—hundreds of miles out of the way—with a connecting flight to Dayton. It was the only way to reach my destination on time.

Instead of being annoyed by the inconvenience, I thanked the Lord for this turn of events and told him I was ready for whatever he had in store for me on this flight. Half-way through a flight I wasn't supposed to be on, a young man tapped me on the shoulder. Immediately I recognized him as someone I had known several years ago.

The young man told me he was on his way to San Diego to begin serving in the Marines.

"I haven't been able to find myself," he said. "So Im going to try to find myself in the marines."

"Kevin," I said, "I have a half hour in Chicago before I catch my next plane, and I'd like to spend that time with you."

"Sure," he said.

We got off the plane, found a place to eat lunch together, and then, I let him have it.

"Kevin," I said, "I can't waste any time. I only have fifteen minutes before my plane leaves, so I want to get right to the point. I want to talk to you about Jesus Christ."

"O.K.," he said. "You know what, somebody just handed me a Bible."

"Show it to me," I said.

He reached in his bag and pulled out a beautiful new Gideon Bible.

"Turn to the last page," I said.

So he turned to the last page, which contained a prayer of surrender to Jesus. The Gideons call it "The Sinner's Prayer," and it is aptly named because all of us are sinners in need of redemption by our Lord Jesus Christ.

"Kevin," I said, "I am now completely out of time. But I want you to do something. When you get to that marine base where you will be staying, I want you to open this Bible and say that prayer every single night until something happens to you.

"And something will happen, Kevin, because Jesus is real. I know he is real and he is the one you are looking for."

Several months later, on Holy Saturday evening, the mailman came to my door and handed me a letter with a Marine Corps return address. On the back of the envelope, on the outside, was written "The Sinner's Prayer." I opened it with eager anticipation and read a note from Kevin: "It's happened to me," he wrote. "Jesus is real! Now I understand what you were trying to tell me in the Chicago airport."

He went on to tell me that he was part of a group of young men on that marine base who prayed together every night before they went to bed.

I was so happy! What a marvelous thing God had done in this young man's life. Because of experiences like that, and I have had many, I no longer worry about missing airplanes, or spending time in waiting rooms, or other similar delays. None of these things need be a waste of my time if I offer that time to the Lord to use as he sees fit.

Anywhere we find ourselves with time on our

hands, even at religious events, there are usually opportunities to witness to someone who needs Jesus Christ in their life. The majority of people around us, including many in our churches and Christian fellowships, need to hear the good news of Jesus Christ.

This is true even of people who have accepted the Lord in their lives. They need encouragement, edification, and fellowship. God can use any Christian who is willing to tell others about the personal love of Jesus Christ.

This is what is called personal evangelism. It is the greatest need in the world today. Millions of people in every nation on earth have not heard or have not believed that the message of Jesus Christ is the message of peace and freedom and joy. They desperately need to hear it, and those of us who have experienced the Lord in our lives are the only ones who can tell them.

Before we can tell them, we must understand clearly what evangelism involves and what the basic message is. While recognizing the pressing needs of the day, many Catholics do not adequately understand what is involved in evangelism. Too many think that evangelization involves some high-powered media campaign which is intended to bring lapsed Catholics back to Mass on Sundays. I am not against such campaigns, but if that is all we are doing, we are not really involved in evangelism.

What is evangelism? Very simply, evangelism involves telling others about how human beings can have a personal relationship with their God in the person of Jesus Christ. Obviously, only someone with a personal relationship with Jesus can evangelize. You can't share something you don't have. So it follows that if you are going to tell others about Jesus Christ you had better know him yourself.

A few years ago Pope Paul VI wrote a document called "Evangelization Today" (in Latin, Evangelii Nuntiandi). It puts the full force of church teaching behind the kind of evangelism that the Lord has called me, and many others, to.

In the first part of that document Pope Paul joyfully repeats a line from one of the documents of the 1974 Synod of Bishops, which also discussed evangelization. It is an exclamation that lays to rest any doubts about what the role of the church is: "We wish to affirm once more that the essential mission of the church is to evangelize all men."

Who is Pope Paul speaking of when he says "the church?" Who are the people who are supposed to be out there every day evangelizing? Who is supposed to be preaching the gospel and leading men and women to make a life-saving commitment to Jesus Christ?

Is it only the job of the bishops, priests, and nuns? Of course not! Every Christian is supposed to be involved constantly in the task of leading others to Christ.

Whenever I speak on this subject, I like to repeat an old slogan I heard somewhere: "Shepherds don't make sheep; sheep make sheep!"

This slogan has an obvious double meaning. It is true both on the biological and spiritual levels. Jesus called the men who were to lead his church shepherds. We continue this tradition down to our age: our pope, our bishops, and our pastors are our shepherds. It is their job, among other things, to preach the gospel to the unconverted. But they can only do so much.

You sheep, on the other hand, live side by side with men and women who have yet to believe the good news. You are the ones that they will listen to most readily. You are the ones who will "make new sheep." You can point the way to Jesus Christ who is always ready, willing and able to set people free.

The Second Vatican Council's Decree on the Apostolate of Lay People puts this same idea in a little more elegant theological terminology:

The laity are made to share in the priestly, prophetical and kingly office of Christ; they have therefore, in the Church and in the world, their own assignment in the mission of the whole People of God. In the concrete, their apostolate is exercised when they work at the evangelization and sanctification of men; it is exercised too when they endeavor to have the Gospel spirit permeate and improve the temporal order, going about it in a way that bears clear witness to Christ and helps forward the salvation of men. The characteristic of the lay state being a life led in the midst of the world and of secular affairs, laymen are called by God to make of their apostolate, through the vigor of their Christian spirit, a leaven in the world. (from section 2)

So there you have it, my brothers and sisters, you who have had a life-changing experience with Jesus Christ. You have been commissioned to go out into the world and tell other people about how they, too, can come to the Lord. Jesus himself tells you to evangelize (see Acts 1:8). The writers of the New Testament epistles tell you to evangelize (see 2 Cor 5:19-21). The Holy Father and the Bishops of the Church tell you to evangelize. What more do you need? People are waiting to hear from you. They know that a lot of things are bad. They're ready for some good news. And Jesus Christ is the good news they are so eager for. Our challenge is to present him in a way that will be believed. This challenge is particularly difficult in our age, lost as it is in skepticism, materialism, and sin. But, the task is not impossible! The Son of God is with us. He has given us his Holy Spirit, and we can do the job because he reigns in our hearts and gives us power. He hungers for souls even more than we do.

Let's talk a little about how to do it. The first thing to realize is that the very heart of the good news is this simple, wonderful fact: the God of this vast creation that we call the universe has chosen to humble himself in order to come and live in the hearts of men and women. We are walking temples of the Holy Spirit. And the simple joy of coming into a personal relationship with Jesus Christ is that we understand this and feel it deeply in every aspect of our lives.

It is important to keep in mind that God loves all people and desires to dwell in their hearts. He wants to be invited into every heart (see Rev 3:20) so he can live there (see Jn 15:23), continually loving and blessing those who invite him in (see Jn 4:13-14; 5:24; 6:35).

The most important thing to communicate to people who do not know the Lord is that Jesus Christ loves them and wants to reign as king in their lives, bringing happiness, peace, and many kinds of blessings. For this to become a reality in their lives, they must humble themselves, recognize their need for God, and say yes to him. Saying yes to Jesus is the key to a full, happy, and fulfilling life.

Our yes to Jesus must be repeated moment by moment and day by day. "Yes, Jesus. I love you. Reign as king in my life today. Fill me with your Holy Spirit, Jesus. Equip me to bear fruit for you. Help me to live today for you and you alone, Jesus."

That, my brothers and sisters, is what life is all about—for newly evangelized people and for us old-timers. We must all recommit ourselves to Jesus Christ day after day, until the very day of our death.

I have had some simply wonderful experiences teaching this to dying people. I served for several years as pastor of St. Joseph's Catholic Church in Little Falls, New York, where I had the opportunity to minister to a number of dying people. I taught them very simply and sincerely to say the most important word anyone can ever say: "Jesus."

They would say, "Jesus, I love you; Jesus, I surrender my life to you." But sometimes dying people are too weak to utter more than one word. What better word for them to have on their lips as they leave this world than, "Jesus, Jesus, Jesus."

I remember a young man who was dying of a terrible sickness called Lou Gehrig's disease. He and his wife had an infant daughter. I had been coming to his home for many weeks, counseling him and his young wife. I prayed with him a number of times and taught him how to surrender his life to Jesus.

One Sunday afternoon I came over to his home. That particular day he was very weak and we all knew that the end of his life was very near.

We prayed with great enthusiasm. This young man, a great big guy, former football player, with trophies all over the room, was laying on his deathbed whispering "Jesus, I love you; Jesus, I love you." As he prayed this way an incredible spirit of peace descended on the room. What joy there was to know that this young man was at peace with his Lord, the Lord who would very soon come to claim him.

After a time of prayer, he whispered in my ear, "Father John, you know what hurts the most? I wish I were able to hold my little girl again."

I sent his wife after the little girl, and we put her on her daddy's chest. I placed one of his arms around the child and the wife placed the other arm around her. It was a sight to see! While he lay there near death, this man was telling his daughter in the only way he could that he loved her and that he knew they would one day be together again.

I was with that young father when he died. It was on the feast of the Holy Family.

He and his wife have taught me more about

commitment and covenant love than I've learned through any formal teaching I've ever received. His wife cared for him in every practical way because his illness left him paralyzed below the neck. The love between them constantly reminded me of the covenanted love Jesus has for his bride, the church. He asked me to be his shepherd for as long as he was alive. Even though I was considering moving to the University of Steubenville, I agreed to remain his parish priest for as long as he lived. He died in December. It was only a few months later; on the anniversary of my baptism in the Holy Spirit, that I clearly knew I was being called forth from the parish to the university.

Spending time at that young man's bedside was perhaps the most rewarding and spiritually enriching experience of my ministry as a parish priest. As he breathed forth his spirit to the Lord, his wife held on to him, gently saying, "I love you John, I love you." I knelt on the other side holding him as his spiritual father, whispering in his ear on his behalf, "I love you Jesus. I love you." To me that moment symbolized the full meaning of Christian family and community: a husband and wife who genuinely love each other in Christ; the presence of a shepherd caring for the flock; the awareness of the centrality of Jesus Christ in every life; the daily surrender to a God who is Lord over life and death.

This is the kind of commitment to which we are all called: to live with peace, joy, and assurance of the love of Jesus in our minds and hearts.It is this same joy and assurance that we are to share with others as we evangelize them.

Many times in our daily lives, the simple, childlike repetition of the name of Jesus can work real miracles for us. Why? Because uttering Jesus' name puts us in the frame of mind necessary to surrender our problems to the Lord. The story of the young man who died with the name of Jesus on his lips is a good example. There is no better way to prepare for death than to repeat the name of Jesus over and over and over.

I like to talk very plainly about death because we are all going to die. I am going to die. You are going to die. When we remember that and prepare for death, it loses its power to make us fearful. Don't wait until you know death is approaching to learn the lesson about repeating the name of Jesus. It has great value every day.

When you are in the hospital, preparing for the surgeon's knife, don't pay attention to all the preparations going on around you. Draw close to the Lord by repeating his name over and over. If you are a married woman, concerned with the care of home and family, don't you have times during the day when you feel like you could climb the walls? Pray the name of Jesus over and over again. Whoever you are, when you are tempted to sin: repeat the name of Jesus again and again. He will come to your aid.

The Bible says, "Draw close to God, and he will draw close to you" (Jas 5:8). That is exactly what I am talking about when I exhort my brothers and sisters to repeat the name of Jesus. This is prayer! This is closeness to God!

What does all this have to do with evangelism?

Plenty. You cannot expect to bear fruit for Jesus Christ, to reach friends and neighbors and other people you feel prompted to evangelize, unless you have—every single day—a vibrant, personal relationship with Jesus. You cannot have that relationship without frequent, simple, prayerful contact with him.

To live a full Christian life requires spending fifteen or thirty or sixty minutes of prayer each day. It also requires spending a few minutes every day reading God's word. Regular fellowship, regular reading of Christian magazines and books, and regular attendance at spiritual events are absolutely essential if you want to grow close to the Lord. But you also need a simple, direct approach to Jesus, one that will bring you into his presence anywhere, anytime, without any preparation, in the midst of a busy life. This is where the repetition of the name of Jesus comes in. Try it and you will see what I mean.

Having this kind of simple closeness with Jesus every day enables us on a moment's notice to share what we have with others. Evangelism then becomes very natural rather than burdensome or awkward. Try it. You will see that it really works!

Reflect once again on the truth of the beautiful teaching of Jesus from John's gospel:

> "I am the true vine
> and my Father is the vinegrower.
> He prunes away
> every barren branch,
> but the fruitful ones

he trims clean
to increase their yield.
You are clean already,
thanks to the word I have spoken to you.
Live on in me, as I do in you.
No more than a branch can bear fruit of itself
apart from the vine,
can you bear fruit
apart from me.
I am the vine, you are the branches.
He who lives in me and I in him,
will produce abundantly,
for apart from me you can do nothing.

(Jn 15:6)

SIX

Called to Be Saints

WE WHO ARE CHRISTIANS belong to a big family, with thousands of years of tradition, and literally thousands of heroic men and women whom we can rightfully claim as ancestors.

Just think of the great Old Testament characters: Moses, Jacob, David, Isaiah, Rachel, Ruth, and Judith. Those men and women are our ancestors in the faith. They believed in God and struggled to live lives worthy of that belief—just like we are doing.

Remember the New Testament heroes: the twelve apostles, Paul, Timothy, Mary, Mary Magdalen, the sisters of Lazarus, Priscilla, and Aquila. And later, the martyrs of the early church: Lucy, Perpetua, Agatha, Stephen, Linus, and hundreds of others.

Moving through the centuries, we have the great teachers and leaders, men and women we call saints today: St. Augustine, St. Benedict, St. Francis, St. Catherine, St. Teresa of Avila, and many others. Let us not forget the modern saintly Christian heroes: St. Maximilian Kolbe, St. Elizabeth Ann Seton, and those thousands of undeclared saints, men and women, who have struggled to keep the faith and pass it on to others.

Yes, we are all part of a glorious family, with a common Father, God himself. All of us are called to a heroic Christian life just as were the great men and women of ages past. All are called to be holy.

Even today there are holy men and women living all around us. There is Mother Teresa, Pope John Paul, and Billy Graham, of course. Such men and women are well-known and honored for their holy lives on behalf of Christ and his gospel. But many thousands of truly holy men and women live alongside us in our prayer groups and parishes. These are the ordinary, everyday saints, men and women standing firm for Christ and his gospel. I meet many of these men and women as I travel throughout the world preaching and ministering the gospel of Jesus Christ. But some of my greatest memories of truly holy men and women come from the fifteen years I spent teaching and ministering in parishes in the Diocese of Albany, New York.

I have already shared some of my experiences as a teacher. Before that time I also served as an assistant pastor. Later, I received my first assignment as a pastor. This was the fulfillment of a dream I had when I first decided to study for the priesthood. In those days, before I knew clearly the kind of ministry the Lord was calling me to, my highest goal was to serve God as a parish priest. Although my only pastorate lasted just four years, it was in many ways a high-point of my priestly life. I would like to tell you a little about those years.

In June of 1976 my bishop appointed me pastor of St. Joseph's Parish in Little Falls, New York, a small town northwest of Albany. St. Joseph's is a typical small-town parish. It contains a mixture of young and old, of townspeople and rural people, and of people with various kinds of philosophies about what parish life should be. St. Joseph's is typical in another way, too. It is filled with men and women who I would call saints—people motivated by the love of Jesus Christ to live good lives every day. Although I was only pastor there for a few years, I was privileged to serve many, many Christian saints.

Earlier I told about the young man from St. Joseph's who died of Lou Gehrig's disease. That young man and his wife, now a widow but very active in the parish, were saintly people in every sense of the word. Through their faith in Jesus and their love for one another, they were able to triumph over disease and death. Because they lived their faith, they experienced the victory of Jesus Christ.

There are other saints in St. Joseph's Parish—men and women who have not experienced anything so dramatic and tragic as a young father's death. These saints are the people who live ordinary lives but live them in the light of faith, doing their best to let the teaching of Jesus, the power of Jesus, and the victory of Jesus motivate their daily lives.

Let me tell you about one of them, a little lady named Pasquilina. She was in her mid-80s when I arrived at St. Joseph's to begin serving as pastor. She had been a widow for a long time. She lived alone and didn't have a lot of money or much education. Yet, what she did have she gave to others generously.

Every noon-time Pasquilina walked into church for daily Mass. The first thing she did was show honor to Jesus and to the Blessed Mother by "throwing a kiss" to a statue of the madonna in the front of the church. She knew, of course, that it was only a statue. But she was doing her best to show Jesus how much she loved him and his mother and how grateful she was for all he had done for her.

Pasquilina's reverence didn't stop with the statue. She would also throw a kiss and a big smile in my direction. She wasn't trying to impress me, or to be cute. She was sincerely showing love to a Christian brother and respect to her pastor, the elder God had placed there to serve her. Pasquilina exuberantly greeted anyone who happened to be in the church at the time.

When someone in the parish died, Pasquilina was always one of the first ones to pay her respects to the bereaved family members. "*Coraggio* (Have courage)," she would say to them in her simple but wise Italian way. Pasquilina wasn't one for emotionalism in such situations. Her simple presence and her simple exhortation, "courage," was a great boost to many a grief-stricken person.

I don't think that Pasquilina had ever heard of the word charismatic. Christian terms like "born again" and "baptism in the Holy Spirit" would have sounded foreign to her. But she did indeed know Jesus Christ in an intimate way. Years before I met her, she had given her heart to Jesus, sold out completely to the Lord and Giver of Life!

Pasquilina's life is ample proof that people who are not involved in the charismatic renewal, or other spiritual movements, can indeed be filled with the Spirit, manifesting his gifts and fruits in their lives. We cannot make the mistake of believing that because other people don't talk or behave the same way we do, that they do not know, love, and serve the Lord.

Pasquilina's life may not sound very saintly, but it actually was. Sanctity consists of doing the best job we can of living the Christian life with the talent, time, and energy God has given us. That is exactly what Pasquilina did. In her simple, loving way she brought joy to many lives, including my own. She loved God with all her heart. She was truly a saint, and I was privileged to be her pastor. Lucky me!

The fact is that Pasquilina was not an exception. I could tell dozens of stories about the men and women in St. Joseph's Parish who served God day in and day out by doing their work, raising their families, and serving the parish in a truly saintly fashion. There are saints in every town, in every parish. All we have to do is look for them, admire them, pray for them, and be inspired by the good things they accomplish for Christ and his church.

During those years at St. Joseph's, I was very happy with my life and ministry as a parish priest. Even so, I was away from town a great deal of the time. Again and again I was called away on speaking engagements. My ministry as an evangelist was in more demand than ever. Everywhere I went I came to know wonderful men and women. I love getting to know people—the challenges of listening, loving and learning from each association, be it brief or enduring, is one of the greatest joys of life.

One man of God who has greatly influenced my life and labors is Bob Cavnar, a retired Air Force colonel. About the same time I was discovering a new dimension of priestly ministry through the baptism in the Holy Spirit and the charismatic renewal, Bob was making similar discoveries for his own life. Today, he is the leader of a large Catholic charismatic community in Dallas, Texas.

In the early 1970s, when his community and my ministry were both getting started, Bob began speaking to me about the gift of inspired preaching. He said that I had that gift and encouraged me to step out in faith and use it, especially for evangelism. He motivated me to reflect prayerfully on the scriptural and historical teaching about evangelistic preaching and to develop the gift God had given me.

I took his advice, first of all by accepting invitations to preach the gospel at prayer meetings and other gatherings. I also discovered that many Catholics who didn't come to the prayer meetings, ordinary Catholics sitting in the pew on Sunday morning, were open to the challenge to accept Christ more fully into their lives. After each sermon, I began to lead people to a personal appropriation of faith in Jesus as Lord and Savior. As I did these two things, I found myself experiencing the ministry of evangelist spoken of in the New Testament.

My role as Catholic evangelist began to increase

the demand for speaking engagements. At first my parishioners in Little Falls accepted my dual role as pastor and travelling evangelist. My bishop had agreed to allow me sixty days a year away from the parish and had given me an associate pastor to help with the work at St. Joseph's. Father Peter McCormick was a real blessing for me personally and an invaluable asset around the parish. So, too, was a Dominican, Sister Prague Maria, who joined our pastoral staff. St. Joseph's parish council and my household staff Mary and Mary Ann also gave me all the help they could.

From my perspective I had the best of both worlds my first several years at St. Josephs. I had an exciting parish ministry with an enthusiastic and supportive parish, and I had increasing opportunities to travel and evangelize. I saw myself as a pretty good pastor-evangelist, and my little flock in Little Falls didn't seem to feel neglected.

But gradually I began to experience what is popularly called "burn-out." I grew tired of trying to be both pastor and evangelist. I was heading for trouble emotionally, physically, and even spiritually. The warning signs began to appear and I recognized them, though not without pain. As the whirlwind of activity increased, I found myself in contact with more and more people looking to me for help and direction at a time when I myself was in desperate need of both.

My internal conflict began to be expressed in ways that were harmful and hurting of others. Finally, through a series of shattering, yet honest, encounters with two members of my congregation who feared for my emotional and spiritual welfare, I was moved to fall on my knees before God and cry out for his direction.

My first thought was to request a year's sabbatical leave. This is a common practice among priests today, and I really was deserving of the time for rest and reflection. My bishop agreed with this assessment and granted the sabbatical. Then he brought up the question of the parish. Would it be right for him to appoint a temporary administrator so I could resume my pastorate after the sabbatical? Or was the Lord calling me to let go of the dream of my life, a parish of the quality of St. Joseph's?

On February 14, 1980, the eleventh anniversary of my baptism in the Holy Spirit, as I knelt before the Blessed Sacrament, worshiping God and awaiting his direction, I received my answer. I had to resign my pastorate and take my sabbatical with total abandonment to the will of the Lord. At this stage of my life, I had to let go of every preconceived notion of what my future should hold. I submitted my life to the Lord and the Franciscan priests at Holy Spirit Monastery in Steubenville, Ohio. I committed myself to a year of living in brotherhood with these men, to resting, praying, and discerning God's will for me.

My only desire was to serve the Catholic Church with the talents and graces that God had given me. I had reached a point where I needed God more than ever, and I needed time to withdraw from both the public spotlight and parochial ministry. In a way, I became, once again, just John Bertolucci, neither pastor nor evangelist, but just plain John, a man who needed to let go and let God take over.

After many tearful farewells, I left the parish of St. Joseph, left my native New York state, and headed toward my first experience of religious life and charismatic covenant community in Steubenville, Ohio.

During that year I accepted some speaking engagements. I also returned to a ministry that I had great love for—working among young people on a college campus. But I devoted myself to prayer, scripture study and meditation as never before. I had the Franciscan brotherhood of Holy Spirit monastery to support me.

By the end of the year my future was laid out as clearly as it could be. The Lord did not want me to return to parish life, but to stay in Steubenville, where I could teach and counsel students, where I could serve and be served by the brothers and sisters in the Servants of Christ the King covenant community, and where my activities as evangelist could be based.

The Franciscan University of Steubenville is a small, Catholic liberal arts college. It sits on a hill overlooking the upper Ohio River Valley which is filled with the steel mills of Steubenville, Ohio, and Weirton, West Virginia. Beyond Weirton, the rolling hills of West Virginia give way to Pennsylvania. Some forty miles away is the city of Pittsburgh.

The University is operated by a branch of Franciscan priests called the Third Order Regulars. Its president is Father Michael Scanlan, who came to the University in 1974 full of fervor because of his involvement in the charismatic renewal. Today, Father Scanlan and eight other Franciscans provide the University with a solid core of Franciscan energy. The University also employs religious sisters and lay men and women as well as diocesan priests like myself.

I had witnessed the Steubenville experience up close for several years because, I was frequently a guest speaker at many of the University's evangelistic conferences for young people, adults, and priests. I had also been advising young people to attend the University, and those who had done so impressed me with their development into mature, productive Christian men and women.

Today, I am an assistant professor of theology at the University. I enjoy my classroom teaching, but my greatest joy is to spend time in one-to-one counseling with the young people at the University. I dearly love counseling, and the Lord certainly seems to bless it. I counsel students about many things: spiritual development, emotional and family problems, career decisions.

One experience that occurred a few months after I arrived at the University illustrates how pervasively the Spirit of Jesus Christ has been allowed to permeate our hilltop. On this particular day I was sitting in my office in Holy Spirit Monastery reading when a student rang the bell. One of the Franciscans answered the door and led the young man inside.

"Father," he said, "The pressure around this place

is beginning to get to me. Everytime I turn around people are talking about Jesus. They all have a relationship with him that I don't share, and I am beginning to feel like an outsider. I've got to get Jesus into my life too."

The priest took care of it right on the spot. He counseled the student and prayed with him, and he did accept Jesus into his life. He left that day a changed young man. Glory be to God! For once peer pressure among young people worked in favor of God's kingdom rather than against it!

Shortly after arriving at the University, I became involved in a new television ministry. Because our program was to be produced in Dallas, I found myself associated with yet another community, the Community of God's Delight, which Bob Cavnar leads. Today I spend approximately two weeks each month in Steubenville, and the other two weeks in Dallas, working on TV programs and living among my brothers and sisters in the community there.

At first I had to be careful that taking on two major ministries—teacher and evangelist—would not result in divided commitments as it had in New York. This did not happen, because the good Lord surrounded me with brothers and sisters in each community who have supported me in every way imaginable. I have been free to pursue my calling as a Catholic evangelist, teacher, and community member because of the support of my committed brothers and sisters.

Both parish life and covenant community life have been very good for me. They continue to serve as vehicles for God to bring men and women to ever-closer relationships with himself. But at this point in my life, covenant community became the situation in which God enabled me to most effectively pursue the ministry he had given me.

SEVEN

The Call to Television

MY DIRECT INVOLVEMENT IN TELEVISION began in 1981. However, the roots of that involvement go back to the mid-1970s when a handful of priests who were serving in the charismatic renewal more or less independently were encouraged to meet together to find ways to support each other.

Bob Cavnar encouraged us to get together. That meeting was held in St. Louis and the priests who attended were among the most influential leaders in the Catholic charismatic renewal at the time.

After that meeting Father Michael Scanlan of Steubenville, and Father James Ferry of Newark, New Jersey, and I decided we should work together in some way. During the next several years, a fellowship developed among the three of us which eventually resulted in my presence at the University of Steubenville. During my first few months at the University, I heard a very clear call from the Lord to become involved in TV evangelism.

Actually, Bob Cavnar had been encouraging me for several years to share my gift of evangelism more widely by taking advantage of radio and television. I had done some media work, but my specific call from God to begin my own television program came as I prayed with my brothers at the Franciscan monastery of the Holy Spirit, begging God's guidance for my life. During those first few months in the monastery, it became increasingly clear that God wanted me to continue my ministry of evangelism. One day, while we were praying, one of the Franciscan priests was inspired to open his Bible to a verse in St. Paul's second letter to the Corinthians:

> For God, who said, "Let light shine out of darkness," has shone in our hearts, that we in turn might make known the glory of God shining on the face of Christ (2 Cor 4:6).

When that passage was read, I was immediately struck by the beauty of its spiritual truth. To think that human beings can make known the glory of God as it shines on the face of Christ! That calls for a sermon on holiness, and, indeed, I have preached on that passage. That day, however, I was struck by the image of the glory of God shining on the face of Christ. It came to me that the television ministry that God was calling me to should draw its name from that passage.

So, we took the word *face* and made it an acronym. The ministry was to be called the St. Francis Association for Catholic Evangelism—FACE. Three of the most important aspects of my life were drawn together in that name: the Franciscan heritage

I received from my grandparents (who were lay Franciscans) and the Franciscans of Steubenville; my beloved Roman Catholic faith; and the call God had given me to be an evangelist.

As I continued to meditate on that passage I also saw in it the actual name of the TV program: "The Glory of God."

I felt strongly that this passage was inspired by the Holy Spirit to apply to my ministry. It was in line with a fundamental principle of evangelism. An evangelist can only teach what comes from his personal faith experience. I can only share with others as much of Jesus Christ as I have personally experienced.

The phrase "shining on the face of Christ" also refers to the church because the church is the body of Christ. We decided that God wanted our program to explain to viewers how the glory of God has been manifest in the Catholic Church in ages past and in our own age. In other words, we saw how we could promote the glory of God by teaching men and women have followed the inspiration of the Holy Spirit.

The scripture verse we received at that prayer meeting tied everything together so neatly, that I believed it just had to be an inspiration from God. And so FACE was born—a ministry which put me in collaboration with the Franciscan University of Steubenville. But next came the question of the technical know-how. How could we actually get the message on TV? Once again Bob Cavnar was the key.

He and the Community of God's Delight in Dallas had been thinking about TV evangelism for quite a while. Together we agreed to cooperate to produce a television program.

We got the ball rolling in early 1981 and our first program went on the air around the time we were celebrating the feast day of our patron St. Francis, October 4, 1981.

The patronage of St. Francis is essential to this project. I insisted from the beginning that it be named in honor of the saint of Assisi for three reasons: Francis was a great evangelist; I was collaborating with a Franciscan community and university; and the ministry should not be something that gave glory to John Bertolucci.

As our name implies, we are an association of men and women who, under the patronage of St. Francis and the inspiration of the Holy Spirit, give glory to God and lead other men and women to know that glory in their own lives.

I am not implying any criticism of well-known evangelists whose ministries are named for them. I have great respect for them and their work. But the Catholic tradition has always been to submerge everything in the church. Francis himself did that. He didn't call his band of followers the Franciscans, that came later, after his death and canonization. He called his troupe of men the Friars Minor, claiming the most lowly title he could think of. Today, many things are named in his honor because of his decision to submit himself and his friars to the church. We gladly submit our association to the church, placing it under the patronage of a great saint of the church.

After producing more than 100 television programs during our first two years, programs which were available in millions of homes, we expanded our ministry to include a weekly radio program. By mid-1984, millions of men and women were able to tune us in either on Christian radio stations or on one of the many cable TV stations that carry our program.

The encouragement I have received from people around the country indicates to me that God is indeed pouring out blessing upon blessing on people because of our programs. Catholics, and many non-Catholics are hungry for the kind of solid spiritual nourishment provided for through FACE.

We have received hundreds of letters from people who have testified that God has blessed them with inspiration, understanding, and healing through our ministry. This is God's doing, not ours. His glory, "shining on the face of Christ" is becoming evident.

Many people tell us that they are returning to the church because of something they heard on the program. Such stories gladden my heart.

Not long ago, after preaching at a parish church in West Virginia, a woman approached me, whose husband had died of cancer a few months before. He had returned to the church and made his peace with God after watching "The Glory of God" on TV.

"You were his constant companion the last year of his life," she told me. "He first heard you when he listened to a tape made at one of your conferences. He liked what you had to say, and when your program appeared on local TV, he watched you every week."

Because of the tapes and the weekly encounter on television, this man gave his life to the Lord, returned to the active practice of his Catholic faith, and was able to face his death with peace and hope.

The man's widow told me that people from the local parish brought him communion every Sunday morning. After receiving communion, he would watch the program.

When she finished, she thanked me and walked away, and I stood there, moved to tears. I never met that man. I was never even in the same room with him. But we were intimately involved with one another, and God allowed me to play an important role in his life. It is stories like this that make the work worth any sacrifice.

More than anything else our television program shows people a side of Catholicism that most of them have never seen before. Many people think of the Catholic Church as a huge institution with many buildings, structures, and rituals, but not much else. They don't see the Christ-centeredness, the heroic holiness, the evangelical fervor that have been part of Catholicism through the ages. We try to show some of this in our programs.

For example, we do our best to show how the Mass and the sacraments are opportunities the church offers to have an encounter with Jesus. Many people have never understood the sacraments this way, so when I present them as Christ-centered, which they really are, people are filled with an understanding and appreciation of the sacraments. I hear many comments along this line. And this also is gratifying.

A great deal of the vision and the hard work which makes the FACE ministry succeed has to be credited to Bob Cavnar and Father Michael Scanlan. As president of the University of Steubenville and leader of the Servants of Christ the King community, Father Michael Scanlan is, in several ways, my boss. But he provides so much more for me than a job. He helps give direction to my life; he helps me discern God's will for me; he offers invaluable advice and counsel. He is a great source of strength and support.

My ministry as an evangelist actually began with personal speaking engagements at various kinds of Christian conferences. Despite the radio and TV ministry, travelling to conferences and other live events is still something I do regularly. I so enjoy meeting God's people and speaking the word the Lord has given me—the good news of salvation and new life in Jesus Christ and the power of his Holy Spirit! Travelling gives me the opportunity to have fellowship with brothers and sisters all over the world.

I had spoken in various places in Latin America, Africa, Europe, Australia, the Philippines, and some cities in Asia. Everywhere I go I see the same kinds of people and hear the same kinds of concerns: men and women are hungry for the word of God. They desire with all their hearts to hear the truth, to make sense of their lives, to overcome their fears and insecurities by turning their lives over to God.

In the past I have been pretty much on my own as I spoke at conferences. I have always submitted my speaking ministry to other Catholic charismatic leaders, and, of course, to my bishop who is my elder in the church. Since I committed my life to a Christian community, I have also been in union with the brothers and sisters in the community. I have also teamed up with Father Michael Scanlan on occasion. But for more than ten years, my normal mode of operation was to minister as an individual preacher.

In the spring of 1983 that changed rather dramatically as I became affiliated in a formal way with three other well-known Catholic teachers in a new ministry, one that I believe will have enormous impact on the church in the future.

EIGHT

FIRE

*"I have come to cast fire on the earth [Jesus said];
and would that it were already kindled."*

(Lk 12:49)

THE SCRIPTURAL IMAGE OF FIRE has always been an
important one for me. From an early age, I was
blessed with a fire of love for the Lord and for his
church. When the Lord favored me with the baptism
in the Holy Spirit, that fire grew into a blaze which
has enabled me to say yes to his plans for my life.

During the first five or six years of my ministry,
the image of God's burning love for his people was
the guiding force in my ministry and in my personal
spiritual development. But during the latter part of
the 1970s the Lord began to show me how the
image of fire refers not only to God's love, but also
to his just demand to be obeyed, to his desire to
remove every obstacle to the spread of the gospel,
and to his determination to cleanse his people from
every stain of evil.

In short, the fire that Jesus speaks of in the passage

from Luke is the fire of God's love for his creation and the fire of his wrath against every force of evil that would try to destroy his creation. I began to understand this better when I came into closer contact with the teaching of Ralph Martin. Ralph is a well-known Catholic layman who teaches and preaches with great wisdom about the Holy Spirit's action in the church today.

Ralph became involved in the charismatic renewal in 1967, when it was just beginning at the University of Notre Dame. Later that year he and three other men established the first covenant community, The Word of God in Ann Arbor, Michigan.

Those of us who follow the Holy Spirit's lead today are indebted to Ralph for his insights into the meaning of God's love and God's judgment in the world today. Ralph's consistent, balanced teaching became more widely known in 1975 through his book *Fire on the Earth*. After I read it, I was determined to allow the fire of God's love to burn even more brightly in my life and to allow the fire of his judgment to cleanse me of the areas of sin that seemed to cling to me.

The teaching of *Fire on the Earth* also took root in the hearts of Fathers Michael Scanlan and James Ferry, the two priests whose ministries and personal friendship had become very important to me. As we continued to find ways to submit to one another for personal spiritual growth, and to cooperate as much as possible in our ministries, we also found ourselves drawn toward Ralph Martin and the brothers and sisters of The Word of God community.

Together with Sister Ann Shields, another long-time collaborator and a well-known spiritual teacher, we decided that God wanted us to share an active and cooperative outreach to Catholics. In 1982, the five of us met in Manhasset, New York, to discuss what form this outreach should take. We also asked several lay men and women whose discernment and collaboration we respected to join us for that meeting.

We prayed and we talked, inspired once again by the scripture passage about fire on the earth. The result of that meeting was the birth of the Catholic Alliance for Faith, Intercession, Repentance, and Evangelism (FIRE).

FIRE is an alliance of four teachers, Father Michael Scanlan, Ralph Martin, Sister Ann Shields, and myself. Father James Ferry and several others have joined us as advisors and staff members. We are also being joined in this alliance by thousands of men and women from throughout the United States and several other countries. In fact, by the end of our first year, 1983, we had approximately 10,000 active members.

FIRE's intention is to spread faith, hope and spiritual renewal among our brothers and sisters in the Roman Catholic Church.

No doubt, that is a tall order. But FIRE has a very specific focus. Our immediate goal is to train Catholic men and women in an ideal of life represented by the four letters of FIRE's acronym. The "F" represents faith in God, his Son Jesus Christ our Lord, and the Holy Spirit. Faith is the starting place

for all spiritual growth. The "I" represents intercession—the faithful, earnest prayer of the people of
God for mercy and blessing upon his people in the
church and upon all mankind in our turbulent
world. The "R" represents repentance, turning away
from those things that separate us from God and
turning toward him in faith, hope and love. The "E"
represents evangelism, the duty every Christian has
to witness to the love of God.

The four teaching members of FIRE explain these
four principles of spiritual growth in talks given at
rallies held in cities throughout North America. For
those who choose to become members, the teaching
is reinforced by additional teaching in the form of
three FIRE publications mailed to members' homes
every other month, and by local activities in some
areas.

During 1983 we conducted three FIRE rallies, all
on the East Coast of the United States. In 1984 the
number of rallies grew to ten and were held in cities
in East and West, North and South, and in Canada
too.

Beause I am the evangelist in the crowd, the talks I
give area always related around the E—evangelism. I
am most comfortable talking about evangelism. Like
everyone else, I need to hear about faith, intercession, and repentance—especially repentance. And
when I hear those three other talks by Ralph, Sister
Ann, and Father Michael, I become a better evangelist.

I could say a lot more about how FIRE works, but
the really exciting thing is that God has used it in

people's lives. We have received hundreds of personal letters testifying to how God has brought peace and healing into some lives, how he has filled others with zeal for spreading the gospel, and how he has enabled others to pray and intercede as never before.

The letters come from ordinary lay men and women—mothers, fathers, single people, teenagers—and from priests and nuns. They tell us that they are indeed growing in faith, intercession, repentance, and evangelism.

I had been a conference speaker for more than ten years when FIRE began in 1983. In fact, I must have spoken at close to 300 such gatherings. At every one of them I have had opportunities to witness God working in profound ways. A very good example of this occurred at our third FIRE rally of 1983, which was held at a large sports arena on Long Island, New York. During my talk on evangelism, I told a story about how God had used a particular event in my life to lead a young man to himself.

It happened this way: One night, when I was still pastor in Little Falls, I was driving on the New York State Thruway. I had been speaking in Western New York and was on my way home. As I was driving, I noticed a young man hitchhiking and I decided to pick him up. I don't always pick up hitchhikers, but on this occasion I sensed that the Lord wanted me to.

I had been listening to Christian music as I was driving, and I kept the music on after my guest was seated and we were on our way. My Bible was also sitting in plain view on the dashboard. So it was obvious to him that I was a Christian, even though I was dressed in casual clothes. He had no idea I was a priest.

"I see you're a Christian," he said.

"Yep, sure am," I answered.

He then proceeded to tell me that he came from a Catholic family, but that he wasn't so sure that he believed in Christianity.

"My mother has been after me to listen to some tapes by some priest with a long, Italian name," he said. "You ever hear of the guy?"

I was quite sure I had. I surpressed a chuckle at God's sense of humor and told him that I was the priest his mother thought he ought to listen to. You can imagine his surprise.

He was a little cautious as we talked, but I shared openly with him about what Jesus Christ meant to me and what he could do in the young man's life. Soon, we came to the place where he had to get out, but before he did, I prayed with him, asking the Lord to come into his life and fill him with the Holy Spirit.

These kinds of things happen to me all the time because I make myself available to the Lord in ordinary kinds of circumstances. At least two of the men on my personal staff are actively involved in Christian community and working full time for the Lord because I obeyed a prompting to reach out and evangelize them. I agreed to be part of the FIRE team because of the urgent need that exists to form men and women into strong and mature Christians.

I believe that the message of FIRE is desperately needed in the world today. It is a message of hope in the midst of a world filled with uncertainty and fear. It is a message of spiritual confidence in the midst of a world filled with spiritual confusion. And it is a message of love—divine and human—in the midst of a world filled with hatred and violence.

There is no need to go into great detail about the obvious problems in the world. Just take a brief look at the many crises we have faced in the last few years: the economic crisis, the energy crisis, the Watergate crisis, the racial tensions, the wars that rage in forty percent of the countries on the face of the earth, the growth of poverty in the third world, the growth of crime and materialism in the wealthy nations, and on and on. As threatening as these crises are, all of them are overshadowed and underscored by the threat of nuclear war.

No wonder the world is so full of confusion and despair! But there is an answer. The way to peace, to lasting solutions to the crises that afflict us, involves faithfully and steadfastly following the straight and narrow road that the holy scriptures and the church set before us. If we are to survive spiritually and physically, we have to know, love, and obey Jesus Christ, the Son of God. We do this by believing, obeying, and proclaiming the full gospel message.

FIRE has been called into being by God so the full gospel can be preached for the salvation of souls and the glory of God in these urgent times.

Some people don't believe that the times we live in are urgent. They say that we have lived through crises before and that we will live through the crises of today. They may be right. Mankind may survive the current worldwide crises and may indeed see a bright, new tomorrow. I hope and pray that we do! But if we do, it will be because Christian men and women, aware of the urgency of the times, fell on their knees in faith, repented for their own sins and the sins of the world, interceded before the throne of the Lamb of God for mercy and grace, and then got up off their knees and set about the work of evangelizing and building a better world.

I am convinced that many people in the world today will be lost for eternity if the people of God, believers throughout the land, do not respond to the warnings God has given us about the significance of the times in which we live. Each of us must turn our life over even more fully to Christ and allow him to set us on fire with zeal for the full gospel message: the message of love and judgment, of mercy and repentance, of intercessory prayer and evangelism.

What are the warnings God has given us? They have come from three sources: from the living word of God in the scriptures; from the teaching of the church through her current leader, Pope John Paul II; and from the special warnings given several times this century in apparitions of the Blessed Virgin Mary.

The writers of the books of sacred scripture warn us again and again of the importance of repentance, of the importance of being faithful to God's times of visitation in our lives, and of the serious consequences that await us if we fail to do so.

John the Baptist prepared the way of the Lord by saying: "I am baptizing you with water, but there is one to come who is mightier than I . . . He will baptize you in the Holy Spirit and in fire. His winnowing-fan is in his hand to clear his threshing floor and gather the wheat into the granary; but the chaff he will burn in unquenchable fire." (Lk 3:16-17) In the next verse Luke adds, "Using exhortations of this sort, he preached the good news to the people."

There is nothing wrong about stressing God's warnings of imminent judgment. The Bible says that such warnings are "good news"; they lead people to make a decision for Jesus or to recommit themselves to Jesus. The whole ministry of Jesus was a visitation from God, a chance for people to repent, to believe the good news, and to give their lives to Jesus. Many did and were spared. Many did not and some of these were lost.

Later in Luke's Gospel, we read of Jesus' lament over his beloved city, Jerusalem, where many had failed to believe and were soon to face the consequences: "If only you had known the path to peace this day; but you have completely lost it from view! Days will come upon you when your enemies will encircle you with a rampart, hem you in, and press you hard from every side. They will wipe you out, you and your children within your walls, and leave not a stone on a stone within you, because you failed to recognize the time of your visitation." (Lk 19:41-44)

How tragic for the people of Jerusalem when,

some thirty-five years later, the armies of Rome did exactly as Jesus had predicted.

In our own century, the very century when the Holy Spirit has been poured out in such abundance, God has given us similar kinds of warnings. The first was in the year 1917 when the Blessed Virgin Mary appeared to a group of children in Fatima, Portugal. This was not the first time God had used Mary to announce his plans for mankind. The first time was when the angel appeared to her and announced that God wanted to plant within her womb the Child who was to be the Savior of the world.

Shortly after the annunciation, Luke tells us, Mary set off to visit her kinswoman Elizabeth. When Elizabeth saw Mary, she reacted with faith. She was able to see God at work, to recognize the visitation of the Holy One, and the child within her own womb, John the Baptist, jumped for joy.

Mary's appearance in Portugal received a similar welcome, at least at first. It happened as World War I was being waged in Europe and just after the Soviet Union had experienced a bloody revolution and was locked in internal struggle and division. Mary told the children that even worse calamities would occur if men and women the world over did not turn from their sinful ways, if the people of God in the church did not offer prayers and sacrifices for sinners.

These calamities would include: another war, more destructive than the present one; great success for Russia in spreading its atheistic errors throughout the world; the annhilation of various nations; the death of many good people; and greater suffering for the Holy Father. Mary asked again for prayer and sacrifice, and, in particular, for the consecration of Russia to her Immaculate Heart to prevent that nation from provoking wars.

Mary promised that a sign would be given to prove that the children were indeed experiencing a visitation from God. That sign was given on October 13, 1917. On that day more than 70,000 people gathered at Fatima. It had rained all night and throughout the morning and the people were all soaking wet. Suddenly, the sun danced in the sky for ten minutes, then plunged toward earth and immediately the whole crowd was dry, as if it had never rained.

The next day, articles about the miracle appeared in newspapers throughout the world. Many reporters had been at Fatima, had seen what God had done. Some of the reporters were avowed atheists; even they had to admit that a great miracle had occurred.

God's warnings through that visitation were obviously not heeded. As Mary predicted, another and much worse world war began two decades later. Russia, indeed, began provoking wars and spreading its atheistic communism throughout the world.

And the Holy Father had much to suffer. In fact, our present Holy Father, suffered an assassination attempt in May of 1980 that almost cost him his life. Yet, exactly one year later, he went to Fatima where he publicly thanked the Blessed Mother for preserv ing his life, and he consecrated the Soviet Union to her Immaculate Heart as she had instructed back in 1917.

Even so, many people have failed to heed the warnings and the world continues to suffer the consequences.

One month after the Holy Father publicly called the attention of the world to the message of Fatima, a group of teenagers in the small town of Medjugorge, Yugoslavia, reported that the Blessed Mother was appearing to them. The message of Medjugorge was very similar to that of Fatima. Through the apparitions, the children said, God was telling the world that a major calamity was imminent unless people repented of their sins and began following the way of Jesus.

The apparitions continued for some time, and I was able to go to Medjugorge to see for myself what was going on. I was impressed by what I saw. I witnessed the children as they saw and spoke with the Blessed Mother. I witnessed the fruit of repentance occurring in the parish community of Medjugorge and in the surrounding area. Although the church has said nothing official about this, and although no final judgment about the authenticity of the apparitions can be made, I came away convinced that God was indeed using the Blessed Mother to speak to the world today.

What is the theme of this time of visitation? The very same message that God has prompted us to preach in FIRE: repent of your sins, recommit yourself to following the way of Jesus, engage in intercessory prayer for the conversion of sinners, and evangelize with fervor so that men and women can come to find salvation in Jesus Christ.

Sacred scripture, Fatima, Medjugorge, God's warnings continue. But who will listen?

The men and women who have chosen to stand with Ralph Martin, Father Michael Scanlan, Sister Ann Shields, and myself have stated their intention to listen to God's warning and claim his promise of mercy. They have chosen to hear what God is saying through us and through his other messengers, especially the Holy Father and the Blessed Mother. They have chosen to allow the teaching of FIRE to continue to form them.

I believe that FIRE will produce great fruit for the Lord in the Catholic Church. Through FIRE, men and women will grow closer to God, and will become effective agents of his renewal in their families, in their parishes, and in the larger community. They will burn with zeal to grow in faith, to intercede, to repent, and to evangelize. They will be helped to stand against the anti-Christ forces today with the weapons of spiritual warfare, which include: "the Sword of the Spirit, the Word of God" (Eph 6:17).

NINE

Knowing God Loves You

I HAVE TOLD A GOOD PART of the story of my life—at least the parts which show of Gods' sovereign intervention. I have also told something about how to begin living, or to renew a commitment to live, a solid Christian life of prayer, service and evangelism. My hope and prayer is that you, have been inspired to open yourself completely to whatever God has in mind for you, right now, at this time of your life.

For those who have not accepted Jesus Christ into your life, God's call is to surrender your life to him. For others, God's call is to seek out a prayer group or community where you can be baptized in the Holy Spirit and live a fuller Christian life. For yet others, his call is for you to learn more about intercessory prayer, personal holiness, or to accept a gift like evangelism. God has spoken. Listen to him; obey him. When you do, your life will change, and you will never regret it.

Before concluding, I would like to tell you what I

think is the essential point to communicate about God. This point is: God loves you and wants you to be eternally happy!

God really does love us—every one of us! It is this basic message that I want to convey everytime I stand at a podium to preach, everytime I stand before a classroom full of college students, everytime I evangelize anyone, and everytime I counsel anyone.

God really does love us all. That is why he created us, and why he has stuck with us even when we have failed him. That is why he sent Jesus and the Holy Spirit into the world. He loves us! He wants us to be able to respond to that love so that we will live this life to the fullest and inherit eternal life.

Men and women today often have a terribly difficult time believing that God really does love them. We live in a world filled with tension, with enormous social problems, and with violence of every kind. Such a climate produces tremendous insecurity, doubt, and, sometimes, despair.

To cope we must have faith in God, believing that he loves us and that he wants to shower that love on us day in and day out. I have surrendered my heart to Jesus time and time again. By remembering that God's love for me is the reason for my existence, I am able to go on. I want to tell the whole world to turn in faith to God. Let God's love fill your heart, your mind, and your soul. Only then can you love God in return. Only then can you love others. Only then can you really even love yourself.

When I talk about love, I am not talking about the

romanticized idea of love that is so common in popular songs and movies. I am not talking about feelings or sexual attachment. The outside world presents these as the elements of love, but they are not the essence of love.

When I use the word *love* I am talking about divine love, about committed, self-sacrificing love. Sure, we often have deep emotions about someone we love. That's only natural. God created those emotions. He also created sexual attachment as an important part of the marriage relationship. But love isn't an emotion, and it certainly isn't sexual activity. It is a personal decision, characterized by commitment, self-sacrifice, and perseverence. This is how God loves us.

God loves us constantly and unendingly, twenty four hours a day, 365 days a year, year after year, as long as we live. God's love surrounds, envelopes, and fills our lives. All we have to do is let him in.

God has provided this kind of committed love for us by giving us Jesus. Jesus is walking with us every precious moment of every day: he is always present, he never goes out for a lunch break, never takes a day off, never abandons us. He simply refuses to walk away from us. He has revealed himself and his Father to us as love.

When you begin to believe that—and it is as true as true can be—it really makes a difference in your life. Why? Because when you believe that God loves you and wants to take care of you, you are always looking for the signs of his activity in your life. You expect him to speak to you. Your expectations will never be disappointed, because God is always active in the lives of those who have given their hearts to him.

The result of experiencing the love of God in our own lives is a new ability to express love to those around us. This involves expressing loving concern for those we live with: spouse, and children, parents, brothers, sisters, roommates, fellow students, and co-workers. As we grow in our ability to receive God's love in our own lives, we also grow in our ability to express God's love in practical ways to others.

If we are not growing in our knowledge of God's love and in our own ability to love, something is very wrong. Why? Because receiving God's love and returning it to him by loving him and loving the other people in our lives is what Christianity is all about. Remember what St. Paul said: "If I do not have love, I am a noisy gong, a clanging cymbal" (1 Cor 13: 1). He meant that if I profess to be a Christian, if I talk about it all the time but do not love God and the others in my life, I am a noisy, useless bag of wind.

Reflect for a moment on the answer Jesus gave to the lawyer who asked a question which was intended to trip him up:

> "Teacher [the lawyer asked], which command-ment of the law is the greatest?"
> Jesus said to him:
> "You shall love the Lord your God
> with your whole heart,

and your whole soul,
and with all your mind.
This is the greatest and first commandment.
The second is like it:
You shall love your neighbor as
yourself." (Mt 22:36-38)

Most of us have heard the sentiments expressed in that passage. We know we are supposed to love God with our whole heart, soul, and mind. But how do we do it?

The most obvious answer is that we grow in love for God by spending time with him in prayer every day. When you love people, you spend as much time with them as possible. You talk to them, listen to them, do things with them. It must be the same in our love relationship with God. We must spend time every day talking to him in prayer, listening to him in contemplation, and discovering more about him by reading scripture and good Christian books and magazines.

The more time we spend with God, the more our love for him will grow and the more we will receive his divine love in our own lives. Love then becomes a cycle. Our capacity to receive and give love grows greater and greater. In fact, our love will never end since we are destined to spend eternity with God and those he loves. Talk about an investment in the future!

Another way to love God with our whole heart and soul and mind is by being grateful for everything he has given us, everything he has done for us. When you consider what God has done for you, you cannot help but be moved to profound gratitude of heart, mind, and soul.

The most significant thing he has done is to become human in order to free us from the curse that our sins have brought on the world. The Creator and Ruler of this vast universe humbled himself and took on the nature of one of his creatures. He became one of us completely, experiencing in his person the same kind of pain, sickness, temptation, and anxiety that we experience. He allowed his own creatures to reject and abuse him, to whip him, to put a crown of thorns on his head in mockery of his kingship, and to hang him on a cross like a criminal to die the most painful death imaginable.

But God didn't stop there. Even though human beings had completely rejected him—except for the handful of men and women who remained faithful to the end—he raised Jesus from the dead, thus defeating death and the forces of darkness, and he sent the Holy Spirit upon all who would believe, thus enabling us to enjoy the benefits he has won for us.

When you think about how profound these actions of God are, you know why the church has always called this the paschal mystery. It is impossible for human beings to completely understand why God would do such a thing. It is especially hard to understand when 2,000 years later, when humanity seems to delight in sin as much as at any time in history.

Yet God patiently waits for us to invite him in. He still pours out love in abundance on all who will call on him in faith, no matter how grievous their personal sins have been. It certainly is a mystery. We cannot understand it, but we certainly can enjoy it!

We have much to be grateful for, and the heartfelt gratitude that comes from meditating on these things is one practical way of returning love to the Lord our God.

As the teaching of Jesus makes so clear, we also love God by loving human beings. Just how do we love those people God places in our lives? I will mention three ways that I believe are especially significant for Christians today. The first involves learning to be servants. The second involves reading the signs that God gives to us in our daily lives. The third involves developing committed relationships with other Christians.

I believe that one of the most significant reasons why God is pouring out his Holy Spirit in the charismatic renewal today is because he wants to raise up a people who are willing to lay down their lives in service to one another. He wants to raise up a people who are not afraid to wash feet, as the master himself did the night before he was crucified.

We who are so richly blessed with spiritual gifts can sometimes get on our high horses, as the old expression goes. We can get carried away with the things God is doing in us and through us, forgetting that one of the most important things we are to do is to perform little acts of love and kindness toward each other. In fact, Jesus says that we will be judged at the end of our lives on how well we served our brothers and sisters. (See Mt 25:34-40).

Because I am so often placed in the role of a celebrity, the "out of town expert" who comes to address thousands of people, I face the high horse temptation rather frequently. One time when this happened the Lord used it to teach me in a very dramatic way how I, too, am called to lay down my life in service to my brothers and sisters.

On this occasion I was one of the speakers at a large conference in Southern California. I was asked to sit on the platform, even though my turn at the podium wasn't to come until later in the day. As I sat there that morning looking out at the men and women who had come to hear the word of the Lord, I noticed a large group of people in wheelchairs right in front of the stage.

My mind wandered for a moment and I thought, wouldn't it be something to step down among them, touch each one and have a bunch of them jump up out of those chairs healed! What a glorious thing that would be.

Well, I quickly rebuked any thought of personal glory. That's not what the Christian life is all about. But I felt impelled by the Lord to step down among them after the morning program ended, to be present to my brothers and sisters, and to see if I could be of some kind of service to them.

As I walked over to them, I began to sense that each of these people, bound as they were in wheelchairs, seemed more full of the presence of God than I did at the moment. I noticed a sparkle in every eye, and even though some had difficulty smiling because of their physical infirmities, I could plainly see the radiance of the love of God on every face. That section of that huge auditorium was simply filled with the power of God and I suddenly knew that I was the one who was being healed, just by being in their presence.

I quickly dropped any delusions I may have had and simply began to enjoy being in their presence, experiencing fellowship with them. But I still felt that I would like to do something for them, so I turned to the Lord in prayer. "Lord," I said, "isn't there something you would have me do for my brothers and sisters here?" I no more than uttered that prayer when I noticed several buckets of fried chicken on the floor. They had been brought as lunch for these people, but the chicken had been left there, and none of these brothers and sisters could feed themselves.

Suddenly it dawned on me why God had called me to be among this group of people. I certainly was to be of service to them, though not in the way I had originally thought. I was to help them eat their lunch.

Well, let me tell you, it was a marvellous experience. I sat there on the floor, in all my clerical glory, breaking off little pieces of fried chicken and placing them in the mouths of the brothers and sisters. The Lord had called me to be a servant; to be of service to his people by laying down my life in a practical way. This is what real love is all about: "As often as you did it for one of my least brothers, you did it for me." (Mt 25:40)

Each of us is called to perform that kind of service to the people God places in our lives every single day. Believe me, most of it is not as dramatic as the story I just told. A wife is called to love her husband by being kind and serving him in practical ways, even when he is grouchy and is not returning her affection. The same is true, of course, for husbands. Parents are called to serve their children in hundreds of ways, and to expect little in return. Each of us have many people we come in contact with every day. We are called to love and serve them, as we are able.

For most of us, being a servant simply means applying the New Testament teaching about loving and serving the people we are in contact with every day in as God-like a way as possible. Jesus showed us how to do that when he washed the feet of the disciples.

The second element in loving others is watching for the signs God gives every day. We Catholics understand the value of signs and symbols. Our liturgical prayer life is filled with ritual signs, taken from the scriptures, which signify God's action among us. The signs I am referring to include the bread and wine of the Eucharist; the water and salt of baptism; the candles that grace the altar every time we worship; and many others.

God sometimes gives us similar kinds of signs in our daily lives. These signs often come to us in the form of gestures of love that we see around us. One such sign occured at a conference where I was speaking.

During one of the sessions, a local man came up to tell the audience about something the Lord had done in the life of his small son. Now I hate to admit it, but I didn't pay too much attention to what the man was saying because I was too busy watching what God was saying through him. You see, the boy had fallen asleep and his father had carried him, very tenderly and carefully, up onto the stage and held him throughout the sharing he was giving.

The scene was so tender, so meaningful, that I couldn't help but be reminded that God relates to each of us in exactly the same way that this father related to his son. He loves us and supports us day in and day out, regardless of how weak or tired we may be. My mind was drawn to the words God spoke to mankind long ago through the mouth of the prophet Isaiah:

> Can a mother forget her infant, be without tenderness for the child of her womb? Even should she forget, I will never forget you.
> See, upon the palms of my hands I have written your name. (Is 49:15-16)

I belive that the example this father was a "sign" from God. God was showing me, and anyone else who had the eyes to notice, his great love. The loving, fatherly action reinforced my belief in God's fatherly love for me, his son. If I were a father, I would have remembered that scene for years. Everytime I had to put up with physical inconvenience for the sake of one of my children, my mind would have returned to that father and I would have found strength.

Many such signs of love are performed around us

every day. God is present in those signs. We should be attentive to them, be inspired by them, and imitate them. This will help us to lay down our lives in love and service of these people God places in our lives.

The third element of loving others involves our need to be supported in our Christian lives by brothers and sisters. We cannot grow in love and service to God and neighbor without being surrounded by deep, loving, committed relationships with brother and sister Christians.

There is no room in the body of Christ for individualism or isolationism. Think, for a moment, of the New Testament account. Jesus founded a church. The men and women who were followers of Jesus in the early days banded around the apostles and shared everything together. They formed a Christian community. St. Paul founded communities of believers wherever he went. The same thing has been true down through the ages: when men and women experience the Lord in a profound, life-changing kind of way, they band together, share life and grow in the Lord together.

This is what we call Christian community, and it is a great need among Christians today, especially among Catholics. One of the biggest problems in the church today is that we have, in many way, abandoned one another. We have allowed ourselves to become too busy or too tired to spend time together. Or we have looked upon spiritual growth as something given to us by the pastors and teachers the church provides for us.

The simple, scriptural fact is that we are responsible for one another. There is no room for individualism or isolationism. We are saved not as individuals but as members of the body; as individuals within the body. We need one another.

I can't lay out a plan which will tell you in full detail how to develop committed relationships with members of your fellowship groups and parishes. The Holy Spirit is the one who creates, builds and sustains Christian community. Individual groups within the body must be attentive to his direction. I do know, however, that community is not an optional extra, like air conditioning in a car. It is a vital element of Christian life. We cannot grow to full stature as Christians without it.

God wants mature men and women in the body of Christ—men and women who know how to love and serve. Christian community, which is characterized by committed relationships, is the way to develop them.

All this talk about love, service, and community sounds like a tall order, doesn't it? How do you go about doing all these things? The place to start is prayer. Ask God to provide you with the inspiration, the energy, and the resources to get started. He will answer that prayer, maybe not in a way that you expected, but he will answer it.

I know that God answers prayers of faith, because he has been answering prayers for me throughout my life. When I was young and my parents, relatives, and the larger church prayed for me, the Lord answered them. As I grew older and learned to pray for myself, the Lord answered those prayers. He has continued to answer prayers throughout my life. This is the only explanation for the multitude of blessings that he has showered on me personally, and on the thousands of people who I have had the privilege of serving.

My final plea to you, my dear reader, is to pray fervently to the Lord. Submit your life to him this day, read his holy word and obey it, call on him for each and every need. He will answer you. He will shower blessing after blessing upon you. And, through his grace, you will join him in his most blessed work of all, spreading the good news in all the world.

Note to the Reader

I HAVE TOLD YOU about the ministries that God has established, and that I am privileged to share in. I recommend that you check your TV listings for the time and channel of "The Glory of God" program. I also recommend that you write to the St. Francis Association for Catholic Evangelism (FACE) and allow us to serve you. In addition to information on our radio and television ministry, I will send you information on FIRE, the Catholic Alliance for Faith, Intercession, Repentance, and Evangelism.

I make this recommendation because I want you to receive the very best support in your walk with the Lord. I also ask for your prayers. There is more I want to share with you; the story is still unfolding for my life and yours as we head toward our eternal destiny in Jesus Christ (Phil 3:12-14).

God bless you.

FACE
P.O. Box 8000
Steubenville, OH 43952